Theater

VOLUME 48, NUMBER 1

T0313406

Tom Sellar, *Editor*

YALE SCHOOL OF DRAMA
YALE REPERTORY THEATRE

EDITOR   Tom Sellar

GUEST COEDITORS *Spectatorship in an Age of Surveillance*   Miriam Felton-Dansky and Jacob Gallagher-Ross

ASSOCIATE EDITOR   David Bruin

MANAGING EDITORS   Michael Breslin, Molly FitzMaurice, and Amauta Martson-Firmino

ADVISORY BOARD   James Bundy, Victoria Nolan, Catherine Sheehy

CONTRIBUTING EDITORS   Una Chaudhuri, Thomas F. DeFrantz, Liz Diamond, Miriam Felton-Dansky, Elinor Fuchs, Jacob Gallagher-Ross, Gitta Honegger, Shannon Jackson, Jonathan Kalb, Renate Klett, Jennifer Krasinski, James Leverett, Mark Lord, Charles McNulty, Tavia Nyong'o, Ken Reynolds, Joseph Roach, Marc Robinson, Chantal Rodriguez, Gordon Rogoff, Daniel Sack, Alisa Solomon, Andrea Tompa, Paul Walsh

AFFILIATED ARTISTS   Marc Bamuthi Joseph, Annie Dorsen, Branden Jacobs-Jenkins, Morgan Jenness, Melanie Joseph, Aaron Landsman, David Levine

Theater is published three times a year (February, May, and November) by Duke University Press, 905 W. Main St., Suite 18B, Durham, NC 27701, on behalf of the Yale School of Drama/Yale Repertory Theatre. For a list of the sources in which *Theater* is indexed and abstracted, see www.dukepress.edu /theater.

SUBMISSIONS AND
EDITORIAL CORRESPONDENCE
See the Duke University Press *Theater* website for detailed submission guidelines: theater.dukejournals.org. Send manuscripts for submission and letters concerning editorial matters to *Theater*, PO BOX 208244, New Haven, CT 06520-8244; theater.magazine @yale.edu.

PERMISSIONS
Photocopies for course or research use that are supplied to the end user at no cost may be made without explicit permission or fee. Photocopies that are provided to the end user for a fee may not be made without payment of permission fees to Duke University Press. Address requests for permission to republish copyrighted material to Rights and Permissions Manager, permissions @dukeupress.edu.

WORLD WIDE WEB
Visit the journal's website at www.theatermagazine.org and Duke University Press Journals at www.dukeupress.edu/journals.

SUBSCRIPTIONS
Direct all orders to Duke University Press, Journals Customer Relations, 905 W. Main St., Suite 18B, Durham, NC 27701. Annual subscription rates: print-plus-electronic institutions, $217; print-only institutions, $206; e-only institutions, $166; e-only individuals, $15; individuals, $30; students, $20. For information on subscriptions to the e-Duke Journals Scholarly Collections, contact libraryrelations@dukeupress.edu. Print subscriptions: add $11 postage and applicable HST (including 5% GST) for Canada; add $14 postage outside the US and Canada. Back volumes (institutions): $206. Single issues: institutions, $69; individuals, $12. For more information, contact Duke University Press Journals at 888-651-0122 (toll-free in the US and Canada) or at 919-688-5134; subscriptions @dukeupress.edu.

ADVERTISEMENTS
Direct inquiries about advertising to Journals Advertising Coordinator, journals_advertising@dukeupress.edu.

DISTRIBUTION
Theater is distributed by Ubiquity Distributors, 607 DeGraw St., Brooklyn, NY 11217; phone: 718-875-5491; fax: 718-875-8047.

© 2018 by Yale School of Drama/ Yale Repertory Theatre
ISSN 0161-0775

Contributors

DAVID BRUIN is a DFA candidate in dramaturgy and dramatic criticism at Yale School of Drama, the associate editor of *Theater*, and the artistic director of un sphinx incompris. As a dramaturg, he is currently working on upcoming projects with Robert Woodruff, Lars Jan, and Lex Brown.

ANNIE DORSEN works in a variety of fields, including theater, dance, and algorithmic performance. Her work has been seen throughout Europe and the United States, including at Brooklyn Academy of Music, Festival d'Automne à Paris, Steirischer Herbst Festival, Holland Festival, Crossing the Line Festival, PS122, and many others. She received an Obie award for her work on the 2008 Broadway musical *Passing Strange*, the 2014 Alpert Award in the Arts, and a 2017 Grant for Artists from the Foundation for Contemporary Arts. She currently teaches in the Theater and Performance Studies department at University of Chicago.

SHONNI ENELOW is an assistant professor of English at Fordham University and the author of *Method Acting and Its Discontents: On American Psycho-Drama* (Northwestern University Press, 2015), for which she won the 2015–2016 George Jean Nathan Award for Dramatic Criticism.

MIRIAM FELTON-DANSKY is assistant professor of Theater and Performance at Bard College and a theater critic for the *Village Voice*. She is a contributing editor of *Theater* and a coeditor of *Theater*'s "Digital Dramaturgies" and "Digital Feelings" issues. Her book *Viral Performance* is forthcoming from Northwestern University Press.

JACOB GALLAGHER-ROSS is assistant professor of English and Drama at the University of Toronto. A contributing editor of *Theater*, he is a coeditor of *Theater*'s "Digital Dramaturgies" and "Digital Feelings" issues. He is the author of *Theaters of the Everyday: Aesthetic Democracy on the American Stage* (Northwestern University Press, 2018).

CADEN MANSON is a director and media artist. He is a founder, along with Jemma Nelson, of Big Art Group, an editor at Contemporary Performance, and the curator for the annual Special Effects Festival in New York City. He has cocreated, directed, media- and set-designed twenty-two Big Art Group productions. For the past sixteen years, Big Art Group has toured throughout Europe and North America and has been coproduced by the Vienna Festival, Festival d'Automne à Paris, Hebbel Am Ufer, Rome's La Vie de Festival, PS122, and Wexner Center for the Arts. Manson is a Foundation for Contemporary Arts Fellow, a Pew Fellow, and a MacDowell Fellow. He has been published in *PAJ*, *Theater Magazine*, *Theater der Zeit*, and *Theatre Journal*. He currently heads the John Wells Directing Program MFA at Carnegie Mellon University's School of Drama.

JOHN H. MUSE is assistant professor in English as well as theater and performance studies at the University of Chicago. His book, *Microdramas: Crucibles for Theater and Time* (University of Michigan, 2017) explores what plays shorter than twenty minutes can teach us about theater's powers and limits. His writing has appeared in *Modern Drama*, *Theatre Journal*, *Journal of American Drama and Theatre*, and *Journal of Dramatic Theory and Criticism*.

JEMMA NELSON is a cofounding member of Big Art Group; has written, programmed, and composed the sound and music for all of Big Art Group's productions; has published writing about performance in *Theater*, *PAJ*, *Theater der Zeit*, and *Mouvement*; received a 2009 fellowship from the Pennsylvania Council for the Arts; and holds an MS in biostatistics.

JENNIFER PARKER-STARBUCK is head of the Department of Drama, Theatre, and Performance, University of Roehampton. She is the editor of *Theatre Journal* and author of *Cyborg Theatre*, coauthor of *Performance and Media: Taxonomies for a Changing Field*, and coeditor of *Performing Animality: Animals in Performance Practices*.

ALEXANDRO SEGADE has presented his series of multimedia science-fiction plays in art and theater spaces, including REDCAT (Los Angeles), Yerba Buena Center for the Arts (San Francisco), Time-Based Art Festival (Portland, OR), and Movement Research Festival (New York). He cofounded the performance art collective My Barbarian in 2001 and is currently working on *The Context*, a graphic novel about pansexual aliens.

TOM SELLAR is editor of *Theater* and professor of dramaturgy and dramatic criticism at Yale School of Drama.

MAURYA WICKSTROM is Professor of Theatre at the College of Staten Island and the Graduate Center, City University of New York. Her most recent essay is "M. Lamar: Singing Slave Insurrection to Marx" (*Theatre Survey*, January 2017). Her third and forthcoming book is *Fiery Temporalities in Theatre and Performance: The Initiation of History* (April 2018).

Contents

Title Page:
Alexandro Segade's
Future St.,
The Fisher Center,
Annandale-on-Hudson,
NY, 2017. Photo: Julieta
Cervantes; courtesy of
Live Arts Bard

Inside Back Cover:
Big Art Group's *Opacity*,
The Fisher Center,
Annandale-on-Hudson,
NY, 2017. Photo: Courtesy
of the artist

Hasan Elahi's *Here v2*,
Follonica, Italy, 2015.
Photo: Courtesy of the artist

Up Front

Citizen Spectators

Tom Sellar, Miriam Felton-Dansky, and Jacob Gallagher-Ross

Mass surveillance conducted by government agencies of their own citizens has turned into one of the twentieth-first century's darkest, if most predictable, realities. Given the long history of wiretaps, illegal searches, and spying by those in power—in democracies and dictatorships alike—no one should have been completely surprised by the 2013 revelations, made by then twenty-nine-year-old National Security Agency contractor Edward Snowden, that supposedly democratic governments (including the United States, the United Kingdom, France, Germany, and others) engage in widespread spying on their own and foreign citizens using telephone and Internet. Snowden's disclosures prompted outrage in the international community and fallout along the political spectrum; they also exposed the dubiety of still-cherished myths about the Internet as a force for social progress and transparency. With Snowden's revelations, the networks we depend on now seem far larger, more totalizing, and less private than previously imagined.

Meanwhile, the ubiquity of mobile devices, the proliferation of social media, and the emergence of sophisticated data-mining techniques have made mass observation by nongovernment actors an inextricable part of the fabric of everyday life. Social media and apps crunching personal data encourage self-surveillance, prompting us to track our every movement and desire—and to passively submit this data to corporations for evermore targeted marketing campaigns—in exchange for sensations of digital connection and communion and new forms of self-knowledge. For some, the intensified scrutiny is productive, even beneficial, allowing us to track steps taken, movies viewed, calories consumed, minutes meditated, and to keep up with distant friends or pursue experiments in self-fashioning. But at other times, we find ourselves assenting to social contracts we don't yet fully understand. Even as we make more and more of ourselves available for others to see, we hide more and more of ourselves behind the delimited forms of communication enabled by digital interfaces. If we're always being watched, and often watching, we're always performing and often spectating—but we frequently

Theater 48:1   DOI 10.1215/01610775-4250912
1

Hasan Elahi's
Sweepback, San Jose
Mineta International
Airport, California,
2009–16. Photo:
Courtesy of the
artist

don't know where one activity ends and the other begins. Foucault's panopticon no longer describes the dispersed power structures organizing surveillance culture. Watchful guards have been replaced by blind algorithms—and by ourselves. As theatermaker Annie Dorsen suggests in these pages, we now find ourselves recalibrating the scale of self, in relation to a digital sublime.

Artists have responded in kind: Hasan Elahi, for example, uses Google Street View to source images for large-scale mounting, alluding to the camera obscura and calling attention to tracking systems that are constantly data-mining the landscapes we live in. Elahi was one of a group of interdisciplinary artists who came together at Live Arts Bard in April 2017 to investigate aspects of surveillance in their projects. Beyond state abuses of technology, privacy, and search and seizure that violate America's Fourth Amendment, what other forms of surveillance have found their way into our lives—online and off? And how might theater and performance, art forms predicated on heightened experiences of viewing—help us to see them?

Bard's performance biennial, titled *We're Watching* and curated by Caleb Hammons and Gideon Lester, set out to answer these questions with a series of commissioned performances in dance, theater, installation, and performance, prefaced with a conference of scholars and artists. Selections from these events appear in this special edition of *Theater*, including essays and documentary traces of the performances. Choreographer Will Rawls and poet Claudia Rankine collaborated on *What Remains*, an exploration of blackness and the gaze. In *Opacity*, Big Art Group contemplates intimacy and queerness experienced through technological metrics and means. *Future St.*, Alexandro Segade's dramatic fantasia, hallucinates a dystopia where desire and gender are closely monitored, but also enhanced by digital connection. These artists are finding new performance languages that embody disparate experiences of pervasive, unbounded surveillance—the kind that transforms bodies and identities into data in real time, all the time. They are asking what it *feels* like to be aware of yourself as alternately (or at once) both a data set and a living body.

This is the final of three editions looking at theater in relation to emerging digital technologies. Like its predecessors—*Digital Dramaturgies* (*Theater* 42:2) and *Digital Feelings* (*Theater* 46:2)—this issue was coedited with contributing editors Miriam Felton-Dansky and Jacob Gallagher-Ross. The articles and projects gathered here help us to understand surveillance, and the impulses it reflects, not only as an anonymous system of digital control and suppression—as it sometimes seems—but more subtly and incisively, as a human behavior enacted by the individual self. Such understandings of the purpose and varieties of surveillance may help us to resist the pervasive spying to which we're fast becoming accustomed.

Samuel Miller's
Foundation for Healing,
The Fisher Center for
the Performing Arts,
Annandale-on-Hudson, NY.
Photo: Julieta Cervantes;
courtesy of Live Arts Bard

Jennifer Parker-Starbuck

Surveilling the Scene

It is easy to question the benefits of a media-saturated society when observing the events unfolding in the US White House since Trump was elected president in 2016. Between watching this president, whose tweets are the most reliable insight into his politics, or seeing viral memes branding alternate truth or fake media over actual truth and diligent reporting, and witnessing threats of foreign surveillance driving unprecedented political action, the world feels upside down—a theatricalized account of what is actually real. But as events such as the firing of FBI Director James Comey in May 2017 and its comparison to events from Richard Nixon's presidency have also shown, surveillance has been a key player for a long time, and like contemporary politics, contemporary theater is also experiencing a new wave of thought around surveillance. As surveillance has become more pervasive, sophisticated, and expansive, it has influenced our physical relationship to technologies such as our smartphones, GPS trackers, drones, and cameras. But, as Elise Morrison has pointed out, it is also shaping our identities:

> Techniques and technologies of surveillance, particularly as they are developed to chart the evolving terrain of the Internet and biometric technologies, have brought with them new layers of complexity with regard to issues of agency, (dis)empowerment, identity, participation, discipline, and desire. Characterized by processes that require self-disclosure as a means of participation, digital culture mirrors recent shifts in the operations of surveillance, wherein the centralized, optical, architectural system of panoptic discipline has given way to more dispersed, (in)dividualized, virtual, and algorithmic modes of control.[1]

Yet, an intellectual awareness of these technologies of surveillance is often connected to the material technologies themselves. A CCTV camera, a low-flying drone, or even the camera staring at you from your computer may be a jolt of recognition that engages thinking around this pervasive subject, but precisely because of its sur-

Theater 48:1 DOI 10.1215/01610775-4250924

reptitious nature, surveillance is more often out of sight and mind. Halfway through Bard College's performance event *We're Watching*, billed as a performance exhibition on surveillance, I had to remind myself that the theme of the day was in fact surveillance. Although I and about seventy others were watching this collection of curated performances and installations, my own spectatorial mode was not at the forefront of my thoughts. Challenging my own expectations about the subject, the day of performance was not replete with CCTV cameras or feeds of people caught on security cameras. Nor did it overtly foreground themes of big data or the politics of tracking devices or drones. Instead, it was a quiet reminder of questions about visibility and invisibility, erasure and opacity, and it spoke to how surveillance in a Big Data society is pervasive to a point of its absorption.

We're Watching took place over the weekend of April 27–30, 2017, but it could also be seen as a one-day "marathon," and from morning to night, from lightness to darkness, and the shades of gray in-between, the full day of performance challenged typical understandings of surveillance and offered deeper insights on how a culture of being watched impacts our physical and emotional makeup. The performance and installations within this curated exhibition, the second edition of the Live Arts Bard (LAB) Biennial, curated and organized by Caleb Hammons and Gideon Lester, took place at Bard's Fisher Center, a gleaming Frank Gehry–designed building in the midst of lush greenery, itself a "theatron" extraordinaire, functioning as a reminder of a relentless state of watching and being watched. Throughout the day performance became an instrumental and resistant reminder that some bodies are watched, scrutinized, and

Surveillance Camera
Players' *God's Eyes
Here on Earth*, St.
Patrick's Cathedral,
New York, 2000.
Photo: Courtesy
of Surveillance
Camera Players

policed more than others. These performances, many still works-in-progress at the time of the event, have taken a while for me to absorb, but they have ultimately challenged my expectations of what surveillance might mean.

The performance exhibition comes at a time when surveillance is a growing topic in theater and performance studies. Elise Morrison's 2016 book, *Discipline and Desire: Surveillance Technologies in Performance*, follows her special guest-edited issue of *International Journal of Performing Arts and Digital Media* (11:2, 2015), "Surveillance Technologies in Performance," and both serve as urgent reminders of this "blind spot" within society, or as James Harding puts it in his article in the special issue, its "amnesiac" effects. Responding to the Surveillance Camera Players' performances with CCTV cameras, he writes that

> CCTV systems have made amnesiacs of us all with regard to our own identities. In the performative acts that they facilitate, acts that, without our consent, cast each and every one of us into sorted categories over which we have little if any control, those systems literally establish who we are and assign us identities of which we can have no recollection because those identities are stored in memory—in data banks—to which we have not been granted access.[2]

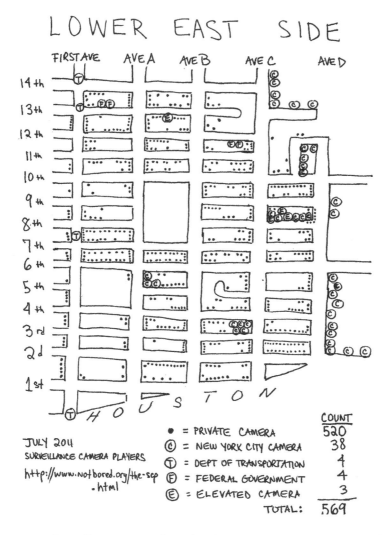

LOWER EAST SIDE

JULY 2011
SURVEILLANCE CAMERA PLAYERS
http://www.notbored.org/the-scp.html

		COUNT
● = PRIVATE CAMERA		520
ⓒ = NEW YORK CITY CAMERA		38
Ⓣ = DEPT OF TRANSPORTATION		4
Ⓕ = FEDERAL GOVERNMENT		4
Ⓔ = ELEVATED CAMERA		3
	TOTAL:	569

Surveillance systems from the ubiquitous CCTV camera to complex facial recognition programs, to algorithms that track our consumer choices, create a moral opacity in our relationship with these technologies of surveillance. Their public acceptance is complexly interwoven with a desire for ease of usage, and despite readily available and frightening statistics covering the proliferation of cameras across the globe, the dependence on our mobile devices is arguably complete. Personally, I admit to being aware of these statistics, and have wondered if my computer is watching me or whether the pop-up ads on my phone indicate the presence of an active listening device. I have followed the Edward Snowden case and have watched a documentary on surveillance that featured a club in Rotterdam at which VIP members could use implanted or cyborgean chips for easier access and drinks purchases,[3] yet I for one also admit to relying on Global Entry and e-passport lines when traveling, and I still maintain several forms of social media (though I have taken to taping over the camera on my computer). This opacity is accepted because it can work both ways, for some. This selective and increasingly problematic "amnesia," a problem communities of color are already acutely aware of—being forced into categories without consent—has become pervasive. As the issues Snowden raised and the recent events in the White House reaffirm, systems of surveillance are also regularly abused.

As a point of resistance and laboratory for possibility, theater and performance are well poised, as Morrison articulates so well in her book, to be bridges between what is and what is possible. Artists such as those invited to participate in this festival, as well as those Morrison covers in her book, begin to allow us multiple focal points through this opaque territory. The commissioned *We're Watching* artists (Big Art Group, Annie Dorsen, Hasan Elahi, Michelle Ellsworth, Claudia Rankine/Will Rawls/John Lucas, Samuel Miller, Alexandro Segade, and their collaborators) sit adjacent to, and develop from, the artists covered in Morrison's book (for example, Essam Attia, Wafaa Bilal, Zac Blas, Edit Kaldor, Jill Magid, The Surveillance Camera Players, among many others); for the artists of *We're Watching*, the issue of "surveillance" often takes a less overt strategy than what might be called the "first wave" of those in Morrison's book.[4] Theirs is also a step further from surveillance-focused work in the 2014 Special Effects Festival by artists David Commander and M. Lamar that Sarah Bay-Cheng covered in *Theater* 44:3—the performances in *We're Watching* function without the technologies themselves as overt coplayers—there were no drones, no actors performing to or through CCTV cameras, no Internet tele-performances.[5] While CCTV cameras and biodata were a focus of at least one performance, the day's events felt more like a meditation on life while under observation. In these performances the ubiquity of surveillance is being absorbed and reflected back through themes of watching and being watched. Although in most instances surveillance technologies are only partially visible if they are visible at all, it is their opacity that these artists are exploring.

Entering and Surveilling the System

As the audience prepared to enter the large inflatable black dome that housed Annie Dorsen's *The Great Outdoors*, I was reminded of the Surveillance Camera Players, whose performances in the late 1990s and 2000s were directed at the people imagined sitting behind public CCTV cameras. The company stood before these cameras and played out classics like *1984* and *Waiting for Godot*, as well as devised works of their own.[6] Holding up signs and engaging passersby, the Surveillance Camera Players imagined a world behind the cameras of those watching, and attempted to remind them that those being watched could also watch back. Dorsen's big black dome, perhaps intended to evoke a planetarium, instead resembled a large CCTV camera, and we were invited in. However, once inside, following instructions to enter one at a time (to avoid "dome collapse"), we found a relaxed environment and sat on padded mats on the floor surrounding a large projector in the center of the dome. While not from a CCTV camera (as I'd hoped), the projections covering the dome exposed a thin strip of ground—a field, a few buildings—and a dome full of bright sky that over the course of the next forty or so minutes shifted from slight cloud differentials to gradual darkness, a blanket of stars and shooting stars, to complete darkness. At one point, as the sky shifted it also made a 360-degree tilt that gave the impression of the world turning upside down. Accompanying the changing sky, a soundtrack became gradually more audible. A lone performer sat amid the audience speaking slowly into a microphone, first words and then phrases that became more complex over time. "No," "Yes," "Maybe," "My Dad," "more Food" became "Live Strong Bracelets," "Damn Girl, good job!," and "Last chance, France," with no apparent connection. Phrases like, "This is gentrified food," "KC and the Sunshine Band: That's the way I like it," turned into longer sentences, and then into mini-monologues about pregnancy, a dog dying, and the possibility of death. A low humming soundtrack under the text that shifted with the sky's changes finally built to a crescendo of sound felt within our bodies. With viewers caught up in the changing sensorial environment, the language began to feel insignificant and as the performer read the random comments and texts, the black sky opened to a small but growing portal of light—a planet or comet slowly growing larger and closer until it "hit" us. Too caught up as we are in the minutia of multidirectional Internet comments, tweets, and texts, we may miss what is in front of us—environmental collapse.

Building on her ideas of "algorithmic" performance, Dorsen has stayed focused on patterns and juxtapositions of random Internet comments (here taken from Reddit), and the piece foregrounds the public nature of casual asides, heartfelt responses, or snarky replies; within this large black dome, we witnessed the circulation of other people's lives and comments. Perhaps we were inside the CCTV camera listening and watching like the National Security Agency (NSA), spies on the snippets and sounds of peoples' daily lives. On the LAB blog accompanying the event, Dorsen responded to Miriam Felton-Dansky in an interview that she wanted the piece to "feel like sitting around a digital campfire," telling stories that were coming from the "cloud."[7] This storytelling begs the questions: What are we listening for and how do we sift through this data? What are the power dynamics of who gets to look out or listen in, and what is done with this information? Will the "cloud," like Dorsen's sky, build to a point of collapse, a complete 360-degree turn? Listening to the sheer randomness and magnitude of the "stories" within this cloud/camera offered a glimpse into the dystopic future-present. In a politically charged moment when who is saying what to whom is driven by clear abuses of power, understanding the sheer magnitude of the outpouring of comments was hard to filter. As surveillance technologies have developed to the point of literally finding a needle in a haystack from miles above, it may be crucial to begin to understand more about the algorithms security companies use to gather intelligence. How much intelligence does it take to find something "meaningful"?

Surveillance takes many forms. If Dorsen's *The Great Outdoors* suggests surveillance writ large, then Michelle Ellsworth's *The Rehearsal Artist* is surveillance writ small. Reminiscent of social science experiments like the Stanford Prison Experiment and the Milgram Experiment, as well as ongoing lab animal testing, this piece interrogated watching and being watched more overtly than others in the festival. Through multiple layers and its playful process, it masks more problematic aspects of the surveillance of individual subjects and produces questions around the anxiety of witnessing. *The Rehearsal Artist* is an installation-performance that walks the audience through a process of surveilling, from the peephole we look through as we walk in (to see an artist sitting with legs crossed painting glaze on what seems to be a stack of donuts; observers might notice that one leg was fake, her real leg exposed behind her), to what could be an experimental or torture device—a large circular wooden wheel within a frame. We are told it is covered in part by one-way glass and we notice that it has a round mirror at the center that, when lit, exposes a white box about a foot and a half square filled with the live head of a performer wearing headphones. The piece is a series of exercises—two bruised arms enter the box through holes on the ceiling and begin to do a series of tasks—filling and then removing a Barbie kitchen set, strewing contents around the small space (hitting the performer at times, feeding her with some of the contents of the kitchen at others), dropping Barbie- and Ken-type dolls into the box

Annie Dorsen's
The Great Outdoors,
The Fisher Center
for the Performing
Arts, Annandale-
on-Hudson, NY,
2017. Photo: Julieta
Cervantes; courtesy
of Live Arts Bard

Michelle Ellsworth's *The Rehearsal Artist*, The Fisher Center for the Performing Arts, Annandale-on-Hudson, NY, 2017. Photo: Julieta Cervantes; courtesy of Live Arts Bard

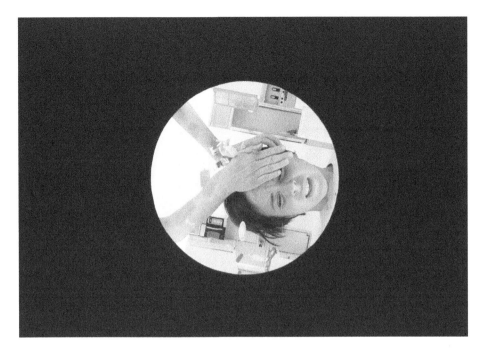

and seating them around the performer, lowering a medical liquid drip bag full of blue liquid into the space and putting the tube into the performer's mouth for her to drink, and so on. During each different exercise the entire wheel turns completely around, and we watch the performer react to being hit by the different objects (the hands attempt to hold on to the more damaging items).

The actions inflicted on the performer make us aware of our status as watchers or observers. What might have at another moment been a test of this complicit status (thinking about Yoko Ono's *Cut Piece*, or Marina Abramović's *Rhythm O*) turns humorous through the use of the props and narrative through the piece. We aren't worried for the performer, really, more curious as to what might fill the space next. Our role as witness is then flipped as we are escorted around to sit behind the device and watch the operation as what appears to be a new group enters the space we vacated. In this segment from behind we are exposed to the inner workings of the piece—Ellsworth is talking to the performer the whole time and giving her a set of instructions. She narrates the actions, telling her what is happening next ("we are going to attach baskets to your legs . . . they are filled with marshmallows . . . you can feel free to touch or throw them.") Ellsworth mitigates the role of the experimenter as controlling or Machiavellian and reminds the performer that if she wants the experiment to stop or it gets to be too much, she can press a button that will shock Ellsworth to alert her (at least we are led to believe she will be shocked). As the device turns its 360-degree rotation and we watch the new group of witnesses, we soon realize they are part of the performance, but before we can understand their role we are escorted out and toward another peephole where Ellsworth is now strapped to another contraption with a mirror attachment through which she can see herself as she maneuvers through the space. As we exit we are given a supposedly defective flip-book of Ellsworth herself as the head in the cube, and the images show her doing a 360-degree turn, upside down and back up again, as we flip through. We are also given our own flip-books—we'd been filmed through a small camera as we watched and were responding to instructions. The accumulation of detritus and props was akin to the accumulation of text in Dorsen's piece. The over-stimulation is perhaps the point—with so much to focus on, how can you know when you are being watched or even what to look for? We were, as well, taken through the experiments as observers but this position as audience-observer was not challenged or shaken, despite the addition of a preshow scenario in which we were asked to provide a swab of our cheek cells and were instructed to affix a strange string of long brown wig hair around any exposed lower legs because they reflected through the one-way mirror. The humorous framing of this performance (and perhaps the always already familiar viewing position of the contemporary Western audience), while it might invoke many scenarios of watching, experimentation, or witnessing, removes the horror and dis-ease we might feel if we watched someone do this to hooded prisoners of war, animals in laboratories, or people targeted unjustly through surveillance technologies.

REMAINS IN THE SYSTEM

When surveillance systems disproportionately target black and minority groups, and the harm done to communities of color is occluded in statistics focusing on surveil-lance's contribution to the "war on terror," one strategy for addressing this violence is to refuse to replicate the technologies of surveillance and to focus instead on the bodies surveilled. Questions of surveillance in *What Remains*, a collaborative piece between Claudia Rankine, John Lucas, and Will Rawls, are then internalized and seem to be waging war within the bodies on stage rather than being imposed from without. This piece comes across as the most explicitly political of the curated works in the event, and it stands out for its racial composition—all performers of color—in, generally speak-ing, a largely white pool of performers and spectators across the day. As the audience was ushered into a cavernous backstage space and watched the loading door slowly roll down to close us in, a sense of being trapped in permeated the space, staging a sensorial feeling to accompany the work that followed. Over the next forty to fifty minutes three performers in long black costumes (Marguerite Hemmings, Jessica Pretty, and Tara Willis) and the sound designer (Jeremy Toussaint-Baptiste) create a sound-poem-dance work that offers a meditation on identity, self-surveillance, and the gray zone between visibility and invisibility.

What Remains attempts to fill a void, the void of the large, white, empty back-stage space, a void left by the erasure of vulnerable communities, a void of bodies taken too early. In an interview with Anna Gallagher-Ross for the Bard Blog that accompanies the performance, Will Rawls explains that "the inspiration for this project is the rather dark desire to contour the space of erasure that is foisted upon people of color across cultural, legislative, and social fields in the US. [We] have been figuring out a way to construct a performance work that can both represent and palpably enact this kind of void."[8] Blending Rankine's ideas and texts from *Citizen* and *Don't Let Me Be Lonely* and Homi Bhabha's *Writing the Void* with a sophisticated, surprising soundscape and unpredictable movement, the piece ricochets through the space, shifting our focus from movement to sound to at one point a black-and-white grainy film projected up in the corner of the back wall. Although Rankine in the same interview refers to a loss of mobility in Trump's presidency—"We want the piece to reflect the deliberate and shameful loss of mobility these human beings are experiencing"—at times Rawls's choreography soared, expressing the inner depths of radically original movement. Bodies stuttered, jolted, and shook, like a record skipping and repeating, or a figure shapeshifting, surveilled from without but remaining resistant within this void.

This piece more than the others produces a question about what vision surveillance produces—the optical illusion of costumes shifting from black to red under different light (evoking the red lights of police cars, the deadly glare of a flash light)—and what, or rather how, we hear—voices rise together in a barely perceptible humming sound that turns to words, "You," the interpellating "Hey You," and phrases, "I don't want nobody fucking with me on the streets," "I'm already dead," to bits of verbal poetry and text to sounds, a long "SSSS" that shifts to "St St St," to a bass sound that reverberates so deeply it physically fills the bodies in the room. It bridged notions of surveillance as discipline with the discipline of bodies remaining despite this relentless gaze. When the performers left through a side door the audience waited for the metal gates to rise before returning to the lobby, remaining for a moment within this "void" to reflect. The audience was offered a performance interpretation of the tension between visibility and invisibility, a sensorial response to the critical question Rawls poses: "When is it important to self-announce in the face of constant erasure and when is it more crucial to remain opaque as a form of resistance to white hegemony that enforces and requires a surveilled transparency at all times?"[9]

SURVEILLING THE FUTURE

What happens to all the data collected about us through our online presence, daily patterns of Internet usage, or our locatable patterns of movement? How have our interpersonal encounters changed through and because of social media? What are the repercussions of this changing, data-connected world? These are some of the questions that are raised and projected into the future by the final two performances of the event: *Opacity*, by Big Art Group (Caden Manson and Jemma Nelson) and *Future St.*, by Alexandro Segade. Creating worlds in which nothing is as transparent as it seems, these pieces

play with our reliance on our digital doubles and ask to what degree this data might already be surveilled by random others, large corporations, and the NSA, as well as where this surveillance unchecked may take us in the future.

We enter into the world of *Opacity*'s two characters through their devices, symbolically projected for us on a large central screen, below which is a black, glossy void. We see: #Searching. #Lonely. #Teenageboredom. The teens sit on either side of the square, texting, lying on or under the table, communicating solely through their phones. We are familiar now with this form of communication and self-surveillance, the selfie, emojis, profile pictures, what we say and do online. With this form of interface frequently replacing real-life interfacial meetings, we see characters "K" and "P" get to know each other, while following the development of their online identities as they "update their profile" and play out a range of typical online scenarios. The now-familiar shortcutting text speak and phrases are juxtaposed with Richard Maxwell–esque songs expressing banal emotional phrases like "Hang on to your heart." As the text develops it appears randomly aggregated, and Manson explains that "each scene is built out of five search terms. We select the five terms, and then we use a Python program to scrape Twitter, which means to collect a thousand recent tweets that use those terms, and then we build the script from that."[10] Like Dorsen's algorithmic developmental explorations, or the NSA finding the needle in the haystack, *Opacity* relies on real comments and usage of the Internet to determine the text for the work. As Manson and Nelson devel-

Alexandro Segade's *Future St.*, The Fisher Center for the Performing Arts, Annandale-on-Hudson, NY, 2017. Photo: Julieta Cervantes; courtesy of Live Arts Bard

oped the piece, they introduced words like *surveillance* and *security* to shape it, creating a surveillance as performance that now drives the internal dramaturgy of the piece.

Playing out their identities more through their exchanges on screen than their face-to-face encounters, the characters are doppelgangers for each other, wearing identical hoodies and jeans, with faces obscured by long brown wigs that completely cover their features. After a period of online courtship, they suggest meeting in person, and after an extended GPS-guided car ride to one of their houses the piece takes a futurist, or perhaps less opaque turn, and the figures end up in the "void" space on stage guided or taken over by the projection of a large 3-D rotating pink figure that looks to be made up of organs or body parts. Although the piece is in development, this shift from the text to a figure on the screen seems crucial to remind users of what lurks behind their screens. As James Harding reminds us, "the real threats from surveillance technologies result not from a centralized government, but rather from the largely unregulated—indeed unregulable—dissemination of surveillance camera technologies into the hands of diverse private commercial and corporate interests."[11] Whether the characters in *Opacity* are encountering a bot like themselves or a more sinister troll is hard to gauge, but regardless there is an eerie tone within the show. The boundary between the familiar, the banal, the everyday, and what lies beneath is opaque but not impenetrable. The innocence and excitement of Internet play and possibility has reached a tipping point, as evidenced in a recent campaign in the UK that has proposed giving those under eighteen the right to have their media fingerprint wiped clean so as to prevent them from future bias.[12]

Big Art Group has been at the forefront of media-based innovation for some time and this piece veers from their usual process, considering the actors more "participants" than performers as they respond to what is being fed to them through earpieces. Manson explained to me, "The performers have in-ear pieces delivering directions and text and monitors downstage have search term–compiled images that they use for choreography. Our new research is very much about networked identity, opacity of the interface, and the lure (ease, connection, identity production) of the surveillance capitalist space (Internet). . . . And the labor we freely give to fuel it."[13] As a form of what I've called elsewhere "karaoke theatre," this mode of channeling, seen more frequently in contemporary performance, reflects on how identities are being shaped by the incessant dataflow we receive on a daily basis.[14] In form as well as content, the piece itself relies on an ever-changing relationship to this "surveillance capitalist space," and reminds us of how complicit we are within this space.

Fans of dystopic film and literature know how often writers and artists have predicted and shaped the technologies of future generations. What was once an anxiety and exhilaration about encroaching technology playing out through lifelike robots and cyborgs has now transformed into scenarios of hackers and cyberterrorism, identity theft, environmental collapse and the end of technology itself, and surveillance. Alexandro Segade's *Future St.* fits securely into a sci-fi genre and is a humorous homage to classic films like *Blade Runner*. The play is also a clever, queer questioning of a techno-logical police state in which male clones have structured what Segade calls "an imaginary gay autocratic state," in which all activities, and even memories, can be tracked by the clone-replicant police. Set in "Clonifornia," *Future St.* stages a queer world in which clones rule and enforce gay marriages, to rebel is to have a girlfriend, and separatists and mothers have formed an underground resistance to resist this monoculture; the main character Sunny is being tracked for his human weaknesses and the data he has disclosed. This sci-fi scenario is classically built around actual anxieties about what data individuals choose to disclose and how it is subsequently used against them.

Well-acted, directed, and designed with an almost sitcom-like polish, the piece uses our familiarity with a futurist sci-fi genre to invert the masculinity of this form but also lets contemporary issues of a surveillance state trouble the sheer fun of the piece. Coming at a time when Margaret Atwood's *The Handmaid's Tale* has just been produced for television, complete with a contemporary tone that decades later still makes this an exemplary and chilling work of science fiction, Segade's piece has fun with things like the gay clone archetype and draws on contemporary themes like gay marriage and surveillance within a not-implausible future run by uncompromising clones (whose rigid ideas at least symbolically evoked some of the current Western political climate). Segade's play entertains what a specific society could become in an age of surveillance—like *The Handmaid's Tale*'s Gilead, *Future St.* also projects a power-based division of culture and society in an already divided world.

This production, alongside the others in *We're Watching*, poses questions that require our complicit behavior—do we vote, for whom, do we make strategic choices, how much data do we contribute to larger data-collection systems, what data is OK to give out publically, what is not, and so on. The success of the Internet and of surveillance relies on our input, and in part on our willingness to be surveilled. As we put more and more data into our devices whether to "like" someone's post, fill out a survey, or just order a new coffeemaker, it is being aggregated and collected. We'd do well to remember that the ease of use could very well lead to a team of replicants chasing us down to wipe our memory! "This is the new amnesia," James Harding cautions; "It is an amnesia of profound political significance because the systems that do remember, that compile information about us and that ultimately construct our identities also determine how we perform in society."[15]

Like theater itself, as Morrison points out so well in her book, surveillance depends on what is unseen. But the value of using performance to situate questions of surveillance is that we are always shifting across these optical registers, watching and being watched. She goes on to explain that "unlike surveillance, which seeks to securely link bodies and objects to their social signs, theatre and live performance require bodies and objects to remain unstable, able to shift between and beyond the materiality they appear to be and the sign to which they refer."[16] This instability may provide a form of resistance to the fixity or assuredness surveillance technologies seem to require. The artists in *We're Watching* foreground our and their bodies over surveillance technologies; domed, dancing, doubled, the bodies are what is at stake in a surveilled society. How, when, and where we are seen may determine our futures. Bodies in performance might challenge this data production. Perhaps this next wave of artists exploring surveillance will also begin to further destabilize any kind of unidirectional viewing system, and like Ellsworth's *Rehearsal Artist*, for example, insist that audiences see from both sides, or in the case of former Bard student Samuel Miller's VR/iPhone installation piece *Foundation for Healing*, begin to explore technologies that allow viewers to better embody the narrative of visual control.[17] These tactics may produce an awareness of the myriad modes through which we are being watched, and offer others to prompt us to look back.

Additionally, curatorial strategies around *We're Watching*—allowing audiences to see works-in-progress, and allowing for an intensive day-long schedule—are reminders of how critical it is to also understand the systems of production around surveillance. For audiences of this event, having the opportunity to examine work that is in progress makes us more open to questions of the fluidity and instability of ideas, identities, images that are too easily understood as fixed. Surveillance systems may be produced to pinpoint individual faces in a crowd, or to raise alerts when "suspicious activity" is noticed, but these systems are not nuanced enough to know when the individual face is an innocent one, or whether what looks suspicious is, in another context, research or humor. The sophistication of surveillance systems is undoubtedly an asset when correctly preventing crime or identifying potential threats; if we could prevent young lives lost outside a pop concert in England or in cities across the Middle East we surely would. But these systems are not fail-safe. Seeing all of the work in *We're Watching* in the one-day marathon form as I did challenged my own viewing processes to find a way to let a sensory overload of material and multidirectional input of ideas that these artists provided be a point of reflection and expansion—like the newly adopted daily data mining for accuracy when sifting through the barrage of news stories, these works become needles in the proverbial haystack to be "surveilled" for more information. Surveillance technologies are only multiplying and growing more sophisticated, and works like these in *We're Watching* serve as questioning interlocutors around narratives on surveillance by foregrounding bodies that question and resist systems that restrict rights and access for so many. The diversity and multi-angled approaches these works provide may force an awareness of and prevent an absorption or normalization of these systems of surveillance.

Notes

1. Elise Morrison, *Discipline and Desire: Surveillance Technologies in Performance* (Ann Arbor: University of Michigan Press, 2016), 9.

2. James Harding, "Outperforming Activism: Reflections on the Demise of the Surveillance Camera Players," *International Journal of Performing Arts and Digital Media* 11, no. 2, (2015): 145.

3. "Science of Surveillance," video, see specifically 38:30 for segment on the Rotterdam Club. www.youtube.com/watch?v=XXIonD93H4Y, accessed May 10, 2017.

4. Of this "first wave" of artists appearing in Morrison's book, Hasan Elahi, whose installation *Retina*, a huge grainy image blown up to the point of misrecognition but also opacity, was also featured in the exhibition at Bard.

5. Sarah Bay-Cheng, "Ready for My Close-Up," *Oakwood Apartments* by David Commander, *Surveillance Project and the Black Psyche* by M. Lamar, Special Effects Festival New York, January 2014 (*Theater* 44, no. 3 [2014]: 86–93). Both performances discussed in Bay-Cheng's essay address questions of surveillance through film, CCTV cameras, and content in ways these performances do not.

6. For more information on the Surveillance Camera Players, see Morrison, *Discipline and Desire*, and Harding, "Outperforming Activism."

7. Annie Dorsen in conversation with Miriam Felton-Dansky, "In Progress: An Interview with Annie Dorsen of The Great Outdoors," *We're Watching* blog, March 15, 2017, blogs .bard.edu/wearewatching/2017/03/15/in-progress-an-interview-with-annie-dorsen-of-the -great-outdoors/.

8. Will Rawls in conversation with Anna Gallagher-Ross, "In Progress: An Interview with John Lucas, Claudia Rankine, and Will Rawls," *We're Watching* blog, February 23, 2017, blogs.bard.edu/wearewatching/2017/02/23/in-process-an-interview-with-john-lucas -claudia-rankine-and-will-rawls-of-what-remains/.

9. Ibid.

10. Interview with Anna Gallagher-Ross, "In Progress: An Interview with Caden Manson and Jemma Nelson of Opacity," *We're Watching* blog, April 6, 2017, blogs.bard.edu /wearewatching/2017/04/06/in-progress-an-interview-with-caden-manson-and -jemma-nelson-of-opacity/.

11. Harding, "Outperforming Activism," 140.

12. See, for example, Nadia Khomami, "Ministers Back Campaign to Give Under-18s Right to Delete Social Media Posts," *Guardian*, July 28, 2015, www.theguardian.com /media/2015/jul/28/ministers-back-campaign-under-18s-right-delete-social-media-posts.

13. Personal correspondence with Caden Manson, May 15, 2017.

14. Jennifer Parker-Starbuck, "Karaoke Theatre: Channelling Mediated Lives," *Contemporary Theatre Review* 27, no. 3 (2017): 379–90.

15. Harding, "Outperforming Activism," 145.

16. Morrison, *Discipline and Desire*, 42.

17. Miller's piece was created for viewing on iPhones, and the work was seen through a cardboard box with VR lenses into which the iPhone was attached. The piece revolved around four stories of individuals attempting to practice self-care in relation to surveillance.

Leos Carax's
Holy Motors, 2012.
Photo: Pierre Grise
Productions

Shonni Enelow

"And If There's No More Beholder?"

Acting and Surveillance

What can we learn from looking at actors about the ways that surveillance has shaped contemporary life?

In Leos Carax's 2012 film *Holy Motors*, a man named Oscar (Denis Lavant) is driven around Paris in a white limousine to a seemingly endless series of appointments. Each appointment, we learn, entails a kind of unframed, or invisibly framed, performance: for the first, Oscar meticulously applies old-age makeup and shrouds himself in rags to become an ancient beggar woman; dropped on a bridge, he begs for change while murmuring in an incomprehensible language. In another, he puts on an orange wig and plays out a surreal scene in Père Lachaise cemetery, hijacking a fashion shoot and kidnapping the model. In a third, he's a scruffy and manipulative father, who picks up his preteen daughter from a party and berates her for being unpopular. Halfway through the film, in between Oscar's appointments, an unnamed man in a suit and sunglasses appears in the limousine with him. "You did a good job tonight," he says.

> MAN: But tell me this. Do you still enjoy your work? I'm asking because some of us think you've looked a bit tired recently. Some don't believe in what they're watching anymore.
>
> OSCAR: I miss the cameras. They used to be heavier than us. Then they became smaller than our heads. Now you can't see them at all. So sometimes I too find it hard to believe in it all.
>
> MAN: Isn't this nostalgia a bit sentimental? Thugs don't need to see the security cameras to believe in them.
>
> OSCAR: Trying to make us all paranoid?[1]

Now that the cameras are invisible, Oscar's relationship to his performances, and the performances themselves, have subtly changed: the imperceptibility of the apparatus of mediation diffuses and attenuates his work. The effect of this unmooring is the collapse of both actor and audience's suspension of disbelief that enables them to invest in the performance; strikingly, here more perceptible mediation means more belief, not less. The conversation aligns these increasingly invisible cameras of our digital mediascape with the hidden cameras of surveillance: according to the unnamed man, surveillance cameras are the model for the invisible cameras that should cause you to believe in your performance even when you can't perceive them, and even when you can't know for sure who, if anyone, is watching.

Linking contemporary media to surveillance, *Holy Motors* highlights their challenges to older aesthetic regimes:

MAN: What makes you carry on, Oscar?

OSCAR: What made me start, the beauty of the act [la beauté du geste].

MAN: Beauty? They say it's in the eye, the eye of the beholder [celui qui regarde].

OSCAR: (off-screen): And if there's no more beholder? [Et si personne ne regarde plus?]

What happens to the actor when "no one" is watching anymore? Is a diffuse, ubiquitous, and insensible watching the same as no watching at all? And is the act (another possible translation would be "the gesture"), and the acting, still beautiful if no one sees it? Is it still an art? The film confuses the boundaries of acting and nonacting throughout: because Oscar's appointments are unframed, there is no way to tell whether his "scene partners" are actors or not. It's unclear, for instance, whether the teenage daughter Oscar picks up from the party has been hired for the role.

I open with *Holy Motors* to point to the ways that surveillance, coupled with the transformations in aesthetic framing due to the ubiquity and miniaturization of photographic media, has changed the work of acting and the way we think about it, in ways that resonate across theater and film. First, it has challenged some long-held assumptions of realist acting, in particular its implicit division of public and private: Konstantin Stanislavsky's ideas about "solitude in public" (translated into American Method acting as "being private in public") depend on the modern assumption of private and public as two separate realms, the former conditioning the latter.[2] Second, it has transformed the aesthetic framing on which the legibility of performance as performance depends, and in the process, cast into question the status of acting as an art. As the man in the suit implies, the photographic capture of film has become more and more like the photographic capture of the imperceptible surveillance cameras that divert criminals, and film acting more like the performance of those would-be criminals, aware that they're being watched without precisely being able to perceive it.

Leos Carax's
Holy Motors, 2012.
Photo: Pierre Grise
Productions

Emily Rosamond has recently argued for "a theory of surveillance scenarios as sites of characterization," highlighting the ways surveillance systems construct subjects as characters through speculative analyses of their behavior. "Acts of characterization," she asserts, "come into play in situations in which the relationship between a person's patterns of action and their motivation comes into question."[3] Although the rest of her essay refers to literary rather than performance theory, the Stanislavskian echoes in her terms defining characterization—*action, motivation*—might suggest that surveillance studies could benefit from a consideration of Stanislavskian and post-Stanislavskian acting, not only to decipher the surveyor's "acts of characterization" of the surveilled subject, but also to read the ways performers engage with or resist such acts of characterization themselves. Such an inquiry would answer Elise Morrison's call to consider the ways that theater both informs and unseats the ideological and disciplinary goals of surveillance: surveillance often constitutes a kind of theater, in which political power aligns with the power to watch, but theater resists efforts to "secur[e] the real," on which surveillance systems depend. Part of the reason for this, as Morrison describes it, is that "whereas prison inmates or 'ordinary practitioners' of surveillance are given to not see certain aspects of surveillance in public space, theater audiences have been conditioned to see double."[4]

The scene from *Holy Motors* with which I began, however, gives us a different view on Morrison's formulation, which leaves out one analogical position: that of the actor. If theater audiences "have been conditioned to see double," and "prison inmates and 'ordinary practitioners'" of surveillance have been conditioned to "not see," what have actors been conditioned to see or not see? In fact, the mediatized surveillance forms that pervade contemporary life more often place us in the situation of the actor than in the situation of the spectator: we are more or less constantly surveilled by visible or hidden cameras in public spaces, by data combers that follow our paths on the Internet, by corporations that buy that data to target our consumption habits, by government agencies that track and record our cell phone usage. It's true that we are also, regularly, surveillers: when we "spy" on a social media account, when we report on suspicious activities in our neighborhoods or mass transit systems, when we view surreptitiously taken images of famous or nonfamous people or take them ourselves. But given that one of these is generally constant, and the other less so, perhaps we should think less about the ways our watching as audience members corresponds or doesn't to the mediated watching of surveillance systems and more about the ways our experiences as surveilled subjects condition our cinematic and theatrical watching. And perhaps we should pay more attention to the experiences of actors as paradigmatic surveilled subjects.

Part of the challenge in writing anything about surveillance is that almost everything can apply: what percentage of our activities are *not* surveilled in some way? We need to take account of the many genres and forms of a surveillance that is multiple, heterogeneous, diffuse. In fact, the pervasiveness and dissemination of surveillance—like the pervasiveness of media—might lead us to questions that are not ontological but affective: not "what is surveillance?" or even "where is surveillance?" but "what feels like surveillance?" This is the stated strategy of John McGrath's *Loving Big Brother*, an early work of surveillance performance studies, which focuses on "the lived experience of surveillance" and works of performance that reflect it.[5] McGrath's study, however, focuses on the experience of theater- and filmgoers, not on how the lived experiences that are presented to them are crafted and embodied.

So how has surveillance affected acting? Rosamond's use of the Stanislavskian terms of action and motivation might be a place to start. It strikes me that, taken as acting theory, these terms sit oddly in a contemporary setting. Elsewhere I have argued that although the language and practices of Stanislavsky-based acting continue to be pervasive in American acting training, they don't square well with the new style of contemporary American film acting I termed "recessive," epitomized by Jennifer Lawrence in *Winter's Bone*, Rooney Mara in *Carol*, Oscar Isaac in *Inside Llewyn Davis*, and Michael B. Jordan in *Creed*. These performances don't conform to the expressive model of repression and release that characterized earlier styles of cinematic realist acting, particularly method acting, which took its psychological models from Freud: instead, they eschew and deflect overt emotional communication. I suggested that this shift indexes a radically transformed notion of trauma—from the unsurpassable event of the past to the everyday precarity and "crisis ordinariness" (as Lauren Berlant terms it) of the present—and also registers, thematically both in many contemporary films' plots, and in their performance affects of suspicion, defensiveness, and watchfulness, a subsumed awareness of and resistance to surveillance.[6]

I would argue that what Rosamond describes as tools for reading character are outdated frames for thinking about contemporary acting, and that their continued usage as surveillance hermeneutics points to a kind of remediation, in Jay David Bolter and Richard Grusin's famous definition, of new media technology representing older forms.[7] If Rosamond's analysis is right, the performance hermeneutics of Stanislavskian realist acting—deciphering action and motivation to craft coherent characterization—are being used in a historical moment in which such forms have, if not entirely gone by the wayside, been thoroughly challenged by the very technologies making it possible for surveillers to deploy them. Arguably, theories of acting have long been in dialogue with technologies of performance capture; Jacob Gallagher-Ross has shown how Lee Strasberg's method acting is dependent on recording technology, not only practically but ideologically: its modes of authenticity, particularly its emphasis on noise over speech, depend on the technological capture of recorded sound.[8] This not only demonstrates that we should think about acting in a landscape of multiple performance media, but also suggests that contemporary performance, live or filmed, carries with it a dialogue about media.[9] The idea that acting indexes contemporary thinking about media jibes with what Martin Harries has recently argued about theater after film: that we should understand it as "a theater made in part of the effects of film."[10] Inverting Bolter and Grusin's definition, Harries asserts that "the 'old' medium . . . may take the newer one as its content."[11] Harries calls the process by which theater took film as its content "dismediation": "remediation through negation of another medium."[12] Extending Harries's argument, we might imagine that today's theater is made in part of the effects of digital media. So thinking through today's media technologies is not only important for a reading of film acting in particular—although we shouldn't assume that it registers them in corresponding or even similar ways; if theatrical acting, like theater, is made in part of the effects of other media, we should be attentive to the ways those other media create pressures that theatrical acting must respond to just as film acting does.

Two performances at Bard's *We're Watching* festival—Annie Dorsen's *The Great Outdoors* and Michelle Ellsworth's *The Rehearsal Artist*—seem to me to offer strong arguments for such an analytical approach. The first, Dorsen's *The Great Outdoors*, might seem an odd work to use to discuss acting. The performance included the live voice of one speaker, but to call her an actor may give pause: sitting cross-legged, like the audience members, in the parachute-style tent we had been led into one by one, she never looked up from the laptop in front of her as she spoke the algorithmically gener-

ated text into a microphone. Her voice began neutrally, with little intonation, as she read the short monosyllables that began her monologue ("No. No. No. No. Right."); at the climax of the piece as the projection tilted and went upside down, her voice became more emotionally expressive, injecting the increasingly, if unevenly, confessional fragments with an urgency that often paired incongruously with the language itself. Most accounts of Dorsen's piece would probably call her "the performer" (as she was listed in the program); a more capacious term, perhaps, than "actor," but also an ideological one, often used to separate experimental or avant-garde theater and performance from more mainstream or traditional forms of theater. Using the word *actor* might therefore direct our attention to the fact that this performance did include some elements associated with the latter: it was a textually based performance, using words not generated by the performer herself, and it did operate with a kind of realism, albeit very different from the psychological models of Stanislavsky and American Method acting. It was realist in the sense that it drew from contemporary life, that it used colloquial language and communication forms, that it included and directed our attention to the material stuff of everyday reality.

I'm skirting a key distinction, however. Was this performance, to use Michael Kirby's terminology from 1972, "matrixed" or "non-matrixed"? I want to briefly turn to Kirby's canonical essay, because I think it shows how the representation frames of performance are currently challenged by the intertwined phenomena of digital media and surveillance. "On Acting and Not-Acting" begins by asserting a basic distinction, drawn from the experimental performance culture of its own moment: the performers of the Happenings were not acting, because "acting means to feign, to simulate, to represent, to impersonate."[13] But his ensuing analysis reveals the difference to be much more subtle. Tracing an "acting/not acting continuum" from "non-matrixed performing," in which a performer, such as a stage attendant in Noh, is "not imbedded, as it were, in matrices of pretended or represented character, situation, place, and time," to "non-matrixed representation," in which a single element, like a costume piece, symbolizes something on the body of the performer with no added effort on her part, to "received acting," which includes more than one theatrical element and so ensures that the performer will be read as a representation of something, despite, again, no work done by him, to "simple acting" and "complex acting," Kirby concludes that "acting can be said to exist in the smallest and simplest action that involves pretense," whether that pretense be a simulated physical action or "merely the 'use' and projection of emotion."[14]

In Kirby's terms, then, the performer of *The Great Outdoors* started out in non-matrixed performance, and began to act (a form of "simple acting") as soon as emotion entered her voice. But I'm not sure this describes my experience of her. In fact, I would submit that *The Great Outdoors* demonstrates how the availability of surveillance data has changed what it means for a performance to be matrixed. Kirby, after all, associates the trend in theater toward less-matrixed performance with the Happenings and "a state of mind that values the concrete as opposed to the pretended or simulated."[15] In contrast, Dorsen's performance values the simulated, challenging, representational matrices in a different way. If, for Kirby, simulation aligns with pretense, impersonation, and feigning, and is separate from the concrete and real, in *The Great Outdoors*, simulation is an intrinsic part of the real. In other words, the simulated, in performance today, is not necessarily matrixed, "imbedded" in pretense. If our perception of

Michelle Ellsworth's *The Rehearsal Artist*, The Fisher Center for the Performing Arts, Annandale-on-Hudson, NY, 2017. Photo: Julieta Cervantes; courtesy of Live Arts Bard

The Rehearsal Artist, 2017. Photo: Julieta Cervantes; courtesy of Live Arts Bard

an event as performance is no longer based on whether or not we perceive it to be simulated—if we no longer receive simulation as intrinsically connected to impersonation or feigning—how does that change our understanding of the continuum of acting and not-acting?

It would be specious to attribute the diverse current forms of nonpsychological acting in both theater and film—many of which, in different ways, reject the "complex acting" tropes of characterization (including arc and journey, subjective consistency, motivation and action)—to the ubiquity of surveillance: for as long as psychological realism has been around, artists have questioned and opposed it on multiple fronts. However, in challenging Kirby's model, *The Great Outdoors* points to several vectors of pressure related to surveillance that contribute to the forms of acting we more often see in experimental theater and performance today, in ways that echo some of the concerns of *Holy Motors*. In addition to subverting the alignment of simulation and performance, Dorsen's piece demonstrated a transformation of ideas about inside and outside. The inside of the tent was encased by a digital projection of a pastoral outdoor scene: a wide field, a night sky, a few structures in the distance. We were inside and outside in the tent, just as we were inside and outside in the text, with weirdly intimate musings (the version I saw included a woman's long discourse on her weight gain during pregnancy) broadcast in the mode of Internet publicity.

I suggested in my reading of *Holy Motors* that the ubiquity and invisibility of cameras has challenged axiomatic assumptions about public and private on which realist acting depends. As Nicholas Ridout argues, we should understand Stanislavsky's interest in privacy on stage in the context of the broader division of public and private life that valorized the authenticity of a private sphere associated with the family home and a corresponding "newly autonomous sphere of . . . feelings."[16] Modern realist acting used the private, a particular historical construction, to signify the interior self, "the autonomous psyche," and, by extension, authenticity and truth. *The Great Outdoors* actively disorganizes this paradigm. In the great outdoors of the Internet, the expanse of digital space made up of expanding particles of attempted communication, we received the actor's text as shooting stars of affect, bursting into the atmosphere and dissipating in long, slowing arcs: psychic space in *The Great Outdoors* isn't the inside, it's the outside, but not as a projection of feeling of an autonomous sphere—as data collection.

Ellsworth's *The Rehearsal Artist* challenged its audience's ability to decipher the matrices of performance in a different way. That Ellsworth's work is typically categorized as dance makes her attention to those matrices, and the recognitions they activate, all the more striking. This was a piece about frames—spherical boxes, peepholes, partitions, and prosceniums—and how they affect the way we read performers. To take our seats, the other audience members and I were ushered into a labyrinthine hallway, encouraged as we did to look through peepholes onto a performer (Ellsworth herself) engaged in an opaque and absurd activity, like a mini-Duchampian assemblage brought to life. We found our chairs in front of a wood partition with two openings in it, the lower one, a spherical box cased in glass, almost the dimensions of a television screen, through which we could see a woman's head, and the higher one, a smaller peephole, through which another woman's face (Ellsworth again) popped through. She spoke directly to us, welcoming us to "the hypothohearsal," and asked us, somewhat uncertainly, to activate our empathy neurons by massaging our faces along with her. Everyone did so. Then she told us that she was going to give "the subject," the head in the box, a series of instructions and disappeared, as two arms invaded the lower box. Although we couldn't hear the words she was saying, we saw the head speaking what looked like emotive language in response to the various recognizable, miniaturized objects the hands dumped in her space: the accoutrements of a dollhouse kitchen; a Barbie-esque wedding; frightening medical equipment. I interpreted these scenes as parodies of traditional realist dramaturgy, the performer trapped and constrained in feminine settings and roles (domestic worker, bride, hysteric). At one point, distressingly, the box rotated, and her head moved upside down, her hair curtaining the sphere, as her face expressed mounting terror. The piece seemed to depict her as a lab rat, a torture victim, a harassed and powerless object of another's fetishistic desires.

And then it stopped. We were instructed to leave our seats and move behind the partition, where we could see from backstage the contraption that made the first performance possible: a giant wheel on which both performers were perched, "the subject" strapped into position and Ellsworth perched above her. We moved to another set of seats and watched a new audience file in through what we could now discern was a two-way mirror. We could now hear what Ellsworth was saying to her fellow performer; to my surprise, she began by telling her that if she (Ellsworth) did anything she ("the subject") didn't like, she could sound an alarm by pushing a button and Ellsworth would stop. The subject wasn't a torture victim; she was consenting to her role. Ellsworth gave her various instructions as she dumped different objects into her case; the subject now seemed a game and flexible actor, in a particularly anxious kind of improvisation exercise. At the close of the performance, as we shuffled out for real, a stagehand gave each audience member a small, bound flip-book made up of photographs of ourselves, massaging our faces at the beginning of the show.

It was a cute trick, more delightful, to me anyways, than unsettling. The gift was accompanied by a tiny baggie filled with yellow dust, with a label announcing it was a fake urine sample. The flip-book and the urine made a strange pair: together they formed a little allegory of coerced consent, inverting my thought process with the piece itself. I began to wonder why it was that I didn't mind the flip-book, but did mind the urine (which I prudishly disposed of as quickly as possible), and realized that I took for granted, going into a public setting, that I would be photographed; and in fact, I was, without my knowledge or permission, by a friend who then posted it on social media. *The Rehearsal Artist* caught me being charmed by my own surveillance: for all its attention to framing, the piece was ultimately less about spectatorship than about the experience of performing, on the part of the audience as well as the actors.

To return to Harries's argument about theater after film: in the postwar era, he argues, in the wake of the widespread sense among both artists and critics that there was something profoundly wrong with mass spectatorship and its modes of identification and subject formation, "the cinematic spectator became the content of theater after film."[17] In contrast, I want to offer the hypothesis that today many works of theater and performance either explicitly or implicitly take as their content the surveilled actor. This is the actor who is unwittingly subjected to the "acts of characterization" (Rosamond) that compose surveillance hermeneutics: the actor that we suspect we all are, we who know we are watched, even if we can't exactly perceive it. Negating these "acts of characterization" and offering other ways to read the actor—as a free/unfree subject (in *The Rehearsal Artist*), as an emotional medium for digital data (in *The Great Outdoors*)—was a way for Dorsen and Ellsworth to think about the experience of being surveilled. Although the Bard festival was called *We're Watching*, none of the pieces I saw were really about the spectator; a better title may have been *We're Watched*.

Notes

1. *Holy Motors*, directed by Leos Carax (Paris: Cinedigm, 2012), video, itunes.apple.com /us/movie/holy-motors/id874175835.

2. See Nicholas Ridout, *Stage Fright, Animals, and Other Theatrical Problems* (Cambridge: Cambridge University Press, 2005).

3. Emily Rosamond, "Technologies of Attribution: Characterizing the Citizen-Consumer in Surveillance Performance," *International Journal of Performance Arts and Digital Media* 11, no. 2 (2015): 151.

4. Elise Morrison, *Discipline and Desire* (Ann Arbor: University of Michigan Press, 2016), 41–42.

5. John E. McGrath, *Loving Big Brother* (London: Routledge, 2004), 2.

6. Shonni Enelow, "The Great Recession," *Film Comment* (Sept–Oct 2016): 56–61. Lauren Berlant, *Cruel Optimism* (Durham, NC: Duke University Press, 2011), 10.

7. Jay David Bolter and Richard Grusin, *Remediation* (Cambridge, MA: MIT Press, 2000).

8. Jacob Gallagher-Ross, "Mediating the Method," *Theatre Survey* 56, no. 3 (2015): 291–313.

9. "Mister Lonely: Interview with Actor Denis Lavant," interview with Louise Catiet, March 19, 2008, franceinlondon.com/en-Article-292-Mister-Lonely-Interview-with -actor-Denis-Lavant-Culture--film-cinema.html.

10. Martin Harries, "Theater after Film: Dismediation," *ELH* 83, no. 2 (2016): 346.

11. Ibid., 349.

12. Ibid., 351.

13. Michael Kirby, "On Acting and Not-Acting," *Drama Review: TDR* 16, no. 1 (1972): 3.

14. Ibid., 4–7.

15. Ibid., 14.

16. Ridout, *Stage Fright*, 45.

17. Harries, "Theater after Film," 352.

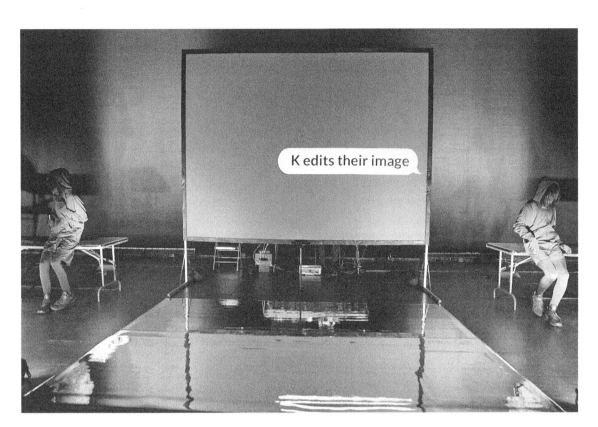

Big Art Group's *Opacity*,
The Fisher Center for
the Performing Arts,
Annandale-on-Hudson,
NY, 2017. Photo: Julieta
Cervantes; courtesy of
Live Arts Bard

Big Art Group

Opacity

System, installation, sound, and text by
Caden Manson and Jemma Nelson

Developed with the Digital Devising Lab
at the Carnegie Mellon University School of Drama:
Caitlin Ayer, Stephen M. Eckert,
Philip Gates, Rachel Karp,
Sara Lyons, Kevin Ramser,
Sylvie Sherman, and Adam Thompson

Note from the Creators

Each of the five scenes in *Opacity* is structured around a 5x5 matrix of search terms (they are projected briefly before each scene; see Table 1 on page 53). Using Python code to search and scrape Twitter, one thousand tweets per search term are compiled into a corpus of about five thousand tweets per scene.[1] The tweet results are minimally cleaned. For text generation, a program using a Markov chain probability function builds the utterances from the corpus of tweets.[2] The performers have in-ear pieces delivering text while video monitors downstage deliver images derived from the same search terms as input for the performer's choreography.

Character actions, feelings, and fears are generated via simple grammar templates that are populated with vocabulary from hand-coded lists; the list elements are sampled randomly according to a uniform distribution.[3] In Scene 3, these stage directions alternate with turn-by-turn-like driving instructions at odds ~2:1 (approximately one-third of the time a driving instruction is supplied, otherwise a stage direction). Each scene restricts stage direction grammars to a subset of several possible grammars contrived for the project. Possible vocabulary items were selected from the Word Associations Network and sentiment/emotion analysis research.[4]—*CM, JN*

Theater 48:1   DOI 10.1215/01610775-4250942
© 2018 by Caden Manson and Jemma Nelson

Scene 1

P and K sit in their own bedrooms swiping through apps

Search Terms: *lonely*, *teenage*, *bedroom*, *phone*, *searching*

Two performers stand in green LED *light leaning against mirrored tables flanking a center stage projection screen and mirrored floor. On the screen, using a messaging interface, speech bubbles appear with the computationally generated character actions text. The performers also receive the text in their in-ear monitors. Images based on the search terms* lonely, *teenage*, *bedroom*, *phone*, *and* searching *are delivered on the downstage video monitors. These images are used by the performers as choreographic input as they execute the character actions simultaneously. The audience witnesses the performers create movement from the video monitors, while embodying the computationally generated character actions.*

```python
#Python code to generate the
character actions text
import random
import inflect
import codecs
import numpy as np

p = inflect.engine()
output = codecs.open('script_
output.txt', 'w', 'utf-8')

# Master list of possible
sentence grammars
SENTENCES = [
['subject','action'],
['subject','echo','object'],
['subject','verb','object'],
['subject','verb','preposition','ar
ticle','adjective','noun'],
['subject','verb','object','preposi
tion','article','noun'],
['subject','verb','object','prep
osition','article','adjective','n
oun'],
['subject','feels'],
['subject','feels','emotion'],
['subject','fears','object']]

# 'part-of-speech' lists for the
grammars
subject = [' P ',' K ',' P and
K ']
action = [' gets up ',' leaves
',' drinks ',' flirts ']
echo = [' echoes ']
verb = [' clicks ',' searches
',' swipes ',' updates ',' edits
',' replies ',' takes ',' asks
',' ghosts ',' changes ',' wants
',' hates ',' likes ',' flirts
',' lurks ',' invites ',' loves
',' needs ',' desires ',' feels
',' fears ',' asks for ']
object = [' coffee ',' K ','
P ',' you ',' me ',' them ','
love ',' sex ',' company ','
loneliness ',' friends ','
openness ',' cautiousness ','
dutifulness ',' self-discipline
',' assertiveness ',' excitement
',' modesty ',' aggression
',' sympathy ',' a message
',' a picture ',' a selfie ','
loneliness ',' intimacy ','
violence ',' people ',' crowds
',' authority ',' information
',' isolation ',' supervision
',' abandonment ',' society
',' outcast ',' abnormality ','
tedium ',' noise ',' enclosure
',' repetition ',' attention ','
interrogation ',' examination
',' curiosity ',' exploration ','
spontaneity ',' oversight ','
friendliness ',' avoidance ','
nothingness ']
```

Opacity, 2017.
Photo: Julieta
Cervantes; courtesy
of Live Arts Bard

preposition= ['to ',' at ',' from ',' by ',' for ',' on ',' through ']
article= [' the ',' a ']
adjective= [' dark ',' dirty ',' scary ',' friendly ',' sexy ',' hopeless']
noun= [' crater ',' bed ',' cafe ',' car ',' home ',' phone ',' hookup ',' selfie ',' shot ']
feels= [' feels ',' hopes ',' doubts ','wonders ',' is ']
emotion= [' lonely ',' nervous ',' -- ',' scared ',' excited ',' attraction ',' sensual ',' dirty']
fears= [' fears ',' dreads ',' avoids ',' deflects ',' shuns ',' escapes ',' fends off ',' ends ',' curtails ',' shuts down ',' veers ',' blocks ',' resists ',' repeats ',' embodies ',' empties ',' abandons ',' casts out ',' isolates ',' separates ',' recoils ',' retreats ',' eludes ',' dissembles ',' hides ',' fakes ',' dissimulates ']
driving = ['Slight left','Do a U-turn','Hard left','Double back','Turn around','Take the on-ramp','Merge','Take the bridge','Take the detour','Descend','Veer','Turn','Continue','Exit']

```
def parsePart(pos):
# For each 'part of speech'
return a random choice from its
list
```

```
        f = ''
        if pos == 'subject':
            f = np.random.
choice(subject)
        if pos == 'action':
            f = np.random.
choice(action)
        if pos == 'echo':
            f = np.random.
choice(echo)
        if pos == 'verb':
            f = np.random.
choice(verb)
        if pos == 'object':
            f = np.random.
choice(object)
        if pos == 'preposition':
            f = np.random.
choice(preposition)
        if pos == 'article':
            f = np.random.
choice(article)
        if pos == 'adjective':
            f = np.random.
choice(adjective)
        if pos == 'noun':
            f = np.random.
choice(noun)
        if pos == 'feels':
            f = np.random.
choice(feels)
        if pos == 'emotion':
            f = np.random.
choice(emotion)
        if pos == 'fears':
            f = np.random.
choice(fears)
        return f


def parseSentence(scene):
# for each sentence grammar,
assemble the parts of speech
# correct for inflections of the
```

```
plural subject (for simple verbs)
# return the assembled sentence
    s = random.choice(scene)
    #print(s)
    ss = ''
    item = ''
    plural_flag = False;
    for pos in s:
        item = parsePart(pos)
        if (pos == 'subject')
and (item.find(' P and K ')==0):
            plural_flag = True
            #print(plural_flag)
        if ((pos == 'verb') or
(pos == 'action') or (pos ==
'feels') or (pos == 'fears')) and
(plural_flag):
            item =
p.plural_verb(item)

#print('pluralverb',item)
        ss += item
    ss=" ".join(ss.split())
    ss+='.  '
    return ss


def
makeStageDirections(scene,scene_
no):
# assembles scenes into a script
    output.write('##############
##########\n')
    output.write('SCENE %s' %
scene_no)
    output.write('\n##########
##############\n')
    line = ''
    for x in range (0,100):
        if scene_no == 3:
            if (np.random.
random()>0.3):
                #print(scene)
                line =
parseSentence(scene)
```

```
        else:
            line = `      •  `
+ np.random.choice(driving)
        else:
            line =
parseSentence(scene)
        output.write(line+'\n')
    if scene _ no == 3:
        output.write(`     • You
have arrived.\n')
    output.write('\n\n\n\n\n')
```

```
SCENE1 =
[['subject','verb','object'
],['subject','action'],[ 'subject','
verb','preposition','article','adje
ctive','noun' ],[ 'subject','verb',
'object','preposition','article','n
oun' ],[ 'subject','verb','object','
preposition','article','adjective',
'noun' ]]
```

###OPACITY

makeStageDirections(SCENE1,1)

(Computationally generated character-actions text is projected inside speech bubbles in a messaging interface on the center stage screen.)

ᴘ fears tedium.

ᴋ likes a picture from a hopeless car.

ᴘ needs sex.

ᴘ and ᴋ update avoidance to a hookup.

ᴋ drinks.

ᴋ clicks avoidance.

ᴘ and ᴋ get up.

ᴘ and ᴋ update by the hopeless shot.

ᴘ loves sex by a car.

ᴘ replies coffee to a cafe.

ᴘ needs violence from a dark cafe.

ᴋ searches curiosity.

ᴋ edits for a hopeless selfie.

ᴋ feels repetition at the dirty home.

ᴘ ghosts for a scary selfie.

ᴘ lurks people on a sexy shot.

ᴋ gets up.

ᴘ needs friends by a friendly selfie.

ᴋ wants modesty by a shot.

ᴋ fears nothingness.

ᴘ asks from the hopeless car.

ᴋ gets up.

ᴘ asks on a hopeless cafe.

ᴘ takes attention through the phone.

ᴘ and ᴋ need a message by a phone.

ᴋ likes avoidance.

ᴘ and ᴋ take supervision through the scary phone.

ᴋ changes sex.

ᴘ and ᴋ drink.

ᴘ flirts attention.

ᴘ feels for the dirty selfie.

ᴋ feels a selfie from a dark phone.

ᴘ and ᴋ want for a dark cafe.

ᴋ drinks.

ᴘ leaves.

ᴋ flirts.

ᴘ and ᴋ hate intimacy at the selfie.

ᴋ invites tedium.

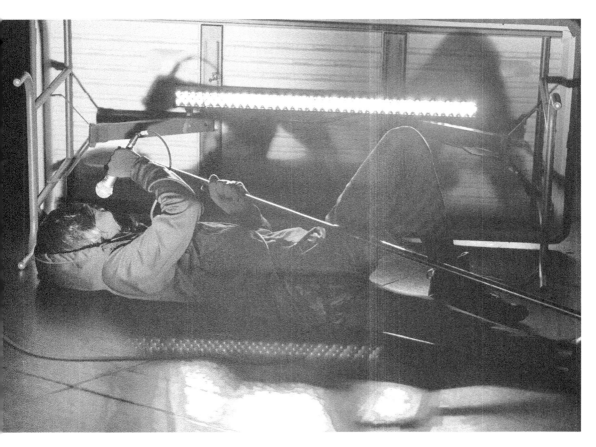

Opacity, 2017.
Photo: Julieta
Cervantes; courtesy
of Live Arts Bard

ᴘ asks for a picture.

ᴘ drinks.

ᴘ feels to the hopeless crater.

ᴘ gets up.

ᴘ and ᴋ love avoidance.

ᴘ invites for a friendly phone.

ᴋ asks for by a hopeless car.

ᴘ and ᴋ click self-discipline.

ᴘ and ᴋ ask assertiveness.

ᴘ and ᴋ get up.

ᴘ and ᴋ leave.

ᴘ flirts.

ᴘ and ᴋ update friends on a home.

ᴋ drinks.

ᴘ and ᴋ asks for by a hopeless selfie.

ᴘ leaves.

ᴋ asks for attention on a car.

ᴋ drinks.

ᴘ and ᴋ swipe spontaneity through a phone.

ᴘ and ᴋ invite to a sexy hookup.

ᴘ and ᴋ search for a dark home.

ᴋ ghosts interrogation.

ᴋ replies a selfie at the scary crater.

ᴘ leaves.

ᴋ edits for a sexy crater.

ᴘ takes on a scary car.

ᴘ leaves.

ᴘ and ᴋ like to a hopeless cafe.

ᴘ and ᴋ ask for from a scary bed.

ᴘ and ᴋ update loneliness at the scary hookup.

ᴋ wants spontaneity from a home.

ᴘ likes by the hopeless home.

ᴘ changes on a scary home.

ᴘ desires company.

ᴘ edits exploration from the scary bed.

ᴘ and ᴋ get up.

ᴘ and ᴋ desire at a scary selfie.

ᴘ and ᴋ click assertiveness through the shot.

ᴘ gets up.

ᴋ loves self-discipline by the cafe.

ᴋ swipes violence from the dirty hookup.

ᴘ and ᴋ love for a sexy home.

ᴘ flirts.

ᴘ leaves.

ᴋ asks for nothingness.

ᴋ swipes to the dark selfie.

ᴋ leaves.

ᴘ loves through a dark car.

ᴋ flirts.

ᴘ and ᴋ flirt cautiousness on a sexy car.

ᴘ and ᴋ search by a dirty home.

ᴘ and ᴋ hate repetition.

ᴋ takes through the scary hookup.

ᴘ and ᴋ ask society from the dirty crater.

ᴘ and ᴋ desire sympathy.

ᴘ updates information from a home.

ᴘ hates sex from a friendly bed.

ᴘ and ᴋ edit avoidance through the home.

ᴘ likes supervision at the hopeless home.

ᴋ feels assertiveness.

ᴋ drinks.

ᴘ leaves.

Sᴄᴇɴᴇ 2

ᴋ meets ᴘ at the Starbucks in the Target at the mall

Sᴇᴀʀᴄʜ Tᴇʀᴍs: *watching, insecure, youth, date, interface*

The two performers meet at the table on stage right in yellow ʟᴇᴅ *light. On the screen, using a photo-sharing interface, computationally generated character feelings are scribbled over searched images of shared Instagram and Snapchat pictures of coffee. The performers receive both the character feelings and procedurally generated dialogue from scraped tweets based on the search terms* watching, insecure, youth, date, *and* interface *through their in-ear monitors. Dialogue filtering has been inverted to allow only emojis to pass through, suppressing non-emoji tokens. Images also based on the search terms are delivered on the downstage video monitors. These images are used by the performers as choreographic input as they execute the text simultaneously. The audience witnesses the performers create movement from the video monitors, while embodying the computationally generated character feelings and speaking the procedurally generated dialogue.*

```
# Code to generate the
character feelings text
# continued from above
```

```
SCENE2 = [['subject','feels'
],['subject','feels','emotion'],['su
bject','feels','emotion','preposit
ion','article','adjective','noun']]
```

###OPACITY
makeStageDirections(SCENE2,2)

(Character-feelings text is scribbled over searched images of shared Instagram and Snapchat pictures of coffee and projected on the center stage screen and in their in-ear monitors.)

P hopes excited.

P is dirty.

P and K feel.

P and K doubt.

P and K feel sensual.

K hopes.

P and K feel dirty through the dirty cafe.

K wonders lonely.

P and K doubt attraction to the sexy bed.

P and K are—.

P wonders.

P and K wonder.

K hopes.

P feels dirty through a sexy shot.

K hopes sensual to a friendly car.

P doubts.

P is.

K is.

P wonders.

P doubts excited from the hopeless hookup.

K wonders sensual through the scary hookup.

P wonders excited.

K doubts—for a hopeless cafe.

P feels.

P hopes.

P and K feel dirty.

P and K hope.

P hopes sensual by a sexy shot.

K is.

K hopes excited from the hopeless shot.

P wonders sensual on a friendly cafe.

P and K wonder scared on a scary phone.

P is attraction for a friendly cafe.

P feels excited for the hopeless car.

P doubts.

P and K doubt.

P and K feel scared through a scary shot.

K is sensual.

K is sensual.

P and K hope.

P and K hope.

K doubts scared.

P hopes lonely on the sexy hookup.

K is.

P hopes.

P and K are.

P and K doubt attraction for the sexy phone.

P doubts attraction.

K wonders.

P and K hope scared.

P and K wonder sensual.

P and K doubt excited on the sexy selfie.

ᴋ is excited.

ᴘ and ᴋ feel.

ᴘ and ᴋ feel attraction.

ᴘ feels.

ᴋ doubts dirty to a friendly shot.

ᴘ hopes sensual.

ᴘ and ᴋ are excited for a dirty home.

ᴘ and ᴋ wonder.

ᴘ and ᴋ hope excited.

ᴘ and ᴋ feel attraction.

ᴘ wonders sensual through the friendly hookup.

ᴘ and ᴋ wonder—at the friendly car.

ᴘ feels sensual.

ᴘ and ᴋ wonder dirty.

ᴋ doubts.

ᴘ and ᴋ feel.

ᴋ doubts.

ᴘ doubts sensual.

ᴋ doubts lonely.

ᴘ feels dirty.

ᴋ wonders attraction at the hopeless selfie.

ᴘ wonders.

ᴘ feels lonely at the scary phone.

ᴘ feels excited.

ᴋ is.

ᴘ doubts attraction.

ᴘ and ᴋ wonder sensual for the friendly car.

ᴘ wonders dirty on a scary selfie.

ᴋ feels lonely through the scary cafe.

ᴘ and ᴋ hope dirty.

ᴋ doubts—.

ᴘ and ᴋ wonder scared at a sexy cafe.

ᴘ hopes.

ᴘ and ᴋ wonder.

ᴘ and ᴋ hope nervous.

ᴘ feels lonely.

ᴘ and ᴋ feel excited.

ᴘ is lonely on the dirty cafe.

ᴋ doubts lonely for the friendly hookup.

ᴋ feels attraction.

ᴘ and ᴋ doubt attraction on a scary crater.

ᴋ wonders.

ᴋ hopes scared through the hopeless crater.

ᴘ and ᴋ hope attraction on the dark cafe.

ᴘ and ᴋ hope.

ᴘ doubts dirty.

ᴘ is attraction.

ᴘ and ᴋ doubt excited.

```
#code to scrape twitter for 5000
tweets (1000 tweets per search
term; watching, insecure, youth,
date, and interface) and to
build the procedurally generated
dialogue for scene 2

import markovify
import codecs
import re
import glob
import time
import random
import sharedfunctions
```

```
NUM _ TO _ GENERATE = 100

MARKOV _ DEPTH = 1

corpus = u""

CLEAN _ TWITTER = True

def cleanCorpusText(text):
    if CLEAN _ TWITTER is True:
        textMod = re.sub("RT ",
rtrepl, text)  # remove RT
        textMod = re.sub("@\w*:
", rtrepl, textMod)  # remove
@:s
        textMod = re.sub("@\w*
", rtrepl, textMod)  # remove
@s
        textMod =
re.sub("https://\S*", rtrepl,
textMod)  # remove links
        textMod =
re.sub("http://\S*", rtrepl,
textMod)  # remove links
        textMod =
re.sub("&amp;", amprepl,
textMod)  # fix &
        textMod = re.sub("&gt;",
gtrepl, textMod)  # fix >
        textMod = re.sub("&lt;",
ltrepl, textMod)  # fix <
    return textMod


class NoTestText(markovify.text.
NewlineText):
    def test _ sentence _
input(self, sentence):
        return True

    def test _ sentence _
output(self, words,
max _ overlap _ ratio,
```

```
max _ overlap _ total):
        return True

for filename in glob.
glob('tweets/*.txt'):
    print "loading " + filename
    with codecs.open(filename,
'rb', 'utf-8') as f:
        text = f.read()
    f.close()
    textMod = sharedfunctions.
cleanCorpusText(text)
    corpus += textMod

if (corpus[len(corpus) - 1] ==
"\n"):
    corpus = corpus[:-1]   #
remove the extra newline at the
bottom.

# save corpus for debug
purposes
textModOut = codecs.
open('corpus.txt', 'w', 'utf-8')
textModOut.write(corpus)
textModOut.close()

text _ model = sharedfunctions.
NoTestText(corpus,
MARKOV _ DEPTH)


print ('---------------')

for i in range(0,
NUM _ TO _ GENERATE):
    # print "time elapsed: " +
str(time.time() - start _ time)
    text _ model
    line = text _ model.
make _ sentence()
```

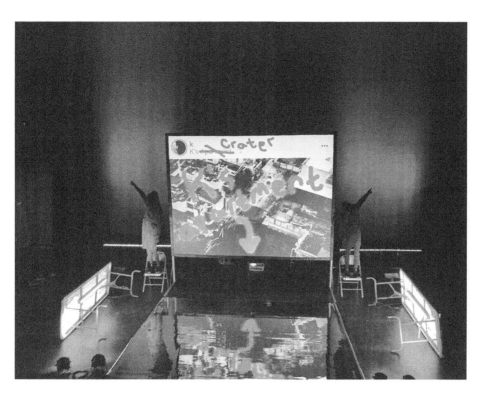

```
    while line is None or
len(line) < 13:
        line = text_model.
make_sentence()
    print(line)
    output.write(line + '\n')
    print ('---------------')
```

```
#For scene 2 a javascript code
is executed to strip the text
and leave only the emojis in
text form.

    var emojiText =
require("emoji-text");
```

```
/*      lineMod = re.sub(" #",
hashtagrepl, line)
        lineMod = re.sub(" lol",
lolrepl, lineMod, flags=re.
IGNORECASE)
        lineMod = re.sub(" lmao",
lmaorepl, lineMod, flags=re.
IGNORECASE)
        lineMod = re.sub(" btw",
btwrepl, lineMod, flags=re.
IGNORECASE)
        lineMod = re.sub(" cya",
cyarepl, lineMod, flags=re.
IGNORECASE)
        lineMod = re.sub("\A#",
hashtagrepl, lineMod)
        lineMod = re.sub("\Alol",
lolrepl, lineMod, flags=re.
IGNORECASE)
        lineMod = re.sub("\
```

```
Almao", lmaorepl, lineMod,
flags=re.IGNORECASE)
      lineMod = re.sub("\Abtw",
btwrepl, lineMod, flags=re.
IGNORECASE)
      lineMod = re.sub("\Acya",
cyarepl, lineMod, flags=re.
IGNORECASE)
*/

// print process.argv
process.argv.forEach(function
(val, index, array) {
  console.log(index + ': ' +
val);
});

var args = process.argv.
slice(2);

var filename = args[0];

var fs = require('fs')
fs.readFile(filename, 'utf8',
function(err, data) {
  if (err) throw err;
  console.log('OK: ' +
filename);
  var lines = data.
split(/\r?\n/);

  var outfile =
fs.open("emojiRevealedOutput.
txt",'w', (err, fd) => {
      for (var i = 0; i <
lines.length; i++) {
            var converted =
emojiText.convert(lines[i], {
            before: ' *',
            after: '* ',
            field:
'description'
         });
```

```
      var split = converted.
split("*");

      converted = converted.
replace(" lol", " L O L ")
      converted = converted.
replace(" lmao", " L M A O ")
      converted = converted.
replace(" btw", " B T W ")
      converted = converted.
replace(" cya", "see ya ")
      converted = converted.
replace("lol ", " L O L ")
      converted = converted.
replace("lmao ", " L M A O ")
      converted = converted.
replace("btw ", " B T W ")
      converted = converted.
replace("cya ", "see ya ")

      var emojiString = "";
      for (var j = 0; j <
split.length - 1; j+=2) {
            var emoji =
split[j+1];
            emojiString +=
emoji + " ";
      }

      if (emojiString.length
== 0) continue;
            console.
log(emojiString);
            fs.write(fd,
emojiString, null, 'utf8');
            fs.write(fd, "\n",
null, 'utf8');
      }

      fs.close(fd);
   });

});
```

(The performers receive the procedurally generated emoji text through their in-ear monitors and whisper them to one another.)

UNAMUSED FACE, CHERRY BLOSSOM, BLUE HEART, FACE THROWING A KISS, WEARY FACE, EYES CRYING FACE CHERRY BLOSSOM BLUE HEART FIRE WEARY FACE SMIRKING FACE CONFUSED FACE PERSON RAISING BOTH HANDS IN CELEBRATION NEUTRAL FACE LOUDLY CRYING FACE THUMBS DOWN SIGN HEAVY BLACK HEART DOUBLE EXCLAMATION MARK, DOUBLE EXCLAMATION MARK, NAIL POLISH, NAIL POLISH, CHERRY BLOSSOM, BLUE HEART, HEAVY BLACK HEART, HEAVY BLACK HEART, HEAVY BLACK HEART, FACE WITH TEARS OF JOY, FACE WITH TEARS OF JOY, YELLOW HEART, FACE THROWING A KISS, CRYING FACE, SMILING FACE WITH SMILING EYES, LOUDLY CRYING FACE, LOUDLY CRYING FACE, LOUDLY CRYING FACE, WEARY FACE, UNAMUSED FACE, HUNDRED POINTS SYMBOL, UNAMUSED FACE, UNAMUSED FACE, FISTED HAND SIGN, FISTED HAND SIGN, FISTED HAND SIGN, LOUDLY CRYING FACE, SNOWFLAKE, BLUE HEART, SNOWFLAKE, WINKING FACE, FACE WITH TEARS OF JOY, SLEEPY FACE, EYES, EYES, TWO HEARTS, TWO BLUE HEART, HAMMER, WRENCH, SOCCER BALL, CHERRY BLOSSOM, BLUE HEART, SMILING FACE WITH HEART-SHAPED EYES, SMILING FACE WITH HEART-SHAPED EYES, SMILING FACE WITH HEART-SHAPED EYES, INFORMATION DESK PERSON, PARTY POPPER, PARTY POPPER, CHERRY BLOSSOM, BLUE HEART, CHERRY BLOSSOM, BLUE HEART, FACE WITH STUCK-OUT TONGUE AND WINKING EYE, HEARTS, TWO HEARTS, TWO HEARTS, SKULL, PURPLE HEART, FIRE, HUNDRED POINTS SYMBOL, PERSON WITH FOLDED HANDS, FACE WITH MEDICAL MASK, HEAVY BLACK HEART, HEAVY BLACK HEART, HEAVY BLACK HEART, FACE WITH TEARS OF JOY, FACE WITH TEARS OF JOY, REVOLVING HEARTS, MONKEY, MONKEY, MONKEY, LOUDLY CRYING FACE, CRYING FACE, HUNDRED POINTS SYMBOL, HUNDRED POINTS SYMBOL, FIRE, MULTIPLE MUSICAL NOTES, FACE WITH TEARS OF JOY, UNAMUSED FACE, FIRE, SMILING FACE WITH HORNS, HUNDRED POINTS SYMBOL, PERSON RAISING BOTH HANDS IN CELEBRATION, WEARY FACE, CHERRY BLOSSOM, BLUE HEART, HEAVY BLACK HEART, SLICE OF PIZZA, UNAMUSED FACE, FACE THROWING A KISS, FACE THROWING A KISS, HEAVY BLACK HEART, HEAVY BLACK HEART, LEAF FLUTTERING IN WIND, ROSE, WEARY FACE, TROPICAL DRINK, COCKTAIL GLASS, WINE GLASS, BEATING HEART, WINKING FACE, CRYING FACE, SMILING FACE WITH HEART-SHAPED. EYES, FACE THROWING A KISS, FACE THROWING A KISS, CHERRY BLOSSOM, BLUE HEART, FACE WITH TEARS OF JOY, LOUDLY CRYING FACE, LOUDLY CRYING FACE, LOUDLY CRYING FACE, LOUDLY CRYING FACE, LOUDLY CRYING FACE, VICTORY HAND, HEAVY MINUS SIGN, EYES, HUNDRED POINTS SYMBOL, OK HAND SIGN, SMILING FACE WITH SMILING EYES, HEAVY BLACK HEART, HEAVY BLACK HEART, HEAVY BLACK HEART, PARTY POPPER, PARTY POPPER, PARTY POPPER, GOAT, SPARKLING HEART, HEAVY MINUS SIGN, CRYING FACE, REVOLVING HEARTS, FACE WITH TEARS OF JOY, FACE WITH TEARS OF JOY, FACE WITH TEARS OF JOY, FACE WITH TEARS OF JOY, FACE WITH TEARS OF JOY, FACE WITH TEARS OF JOY, FACE WITH TEARS OF JOY, FACE WITH TEARS OF JOY, FACE WITH TEARS OF JOY, FACE WITH TEARS OF JOY, FLEXED BICEPS, UNAMUSED FACE, SMILING FACE WITH OPEN MOUTH AND SMILING EYES, AMBULANCE, CHERRY BLOSSOM, BLUE HEART, BROKEN HEART, FACE WITH TEARS OF JOY, TWO HEARTS, TWO HEARTS, TWO HEARTS, CRYING FACE, SMILING FACE WITH HEART-SHAPED EYES, FACE THROWING A KISS, FACE THROWING A KISS, FACE WITH TEARS OF

Opacity, 2017.
Photo: Courtesy
of the artist

JOY, FACE WITH TEARS OF JOY, WINKING FACE, SMILING FACE WITH OPEN MOUTH, CHERRY BLOSSOM, BLUE HEART, SMIRKING FACE, WATER WAVE, HEAVY MINUS SIGN, SMILING FACE WITH SUNGLASSES, FACE WITH TEARS OF JOY, EYES, CHERRY BLOSSOM, BLUE HEART, FACE WITH TEARS OF JOY, WEARY FACE.

SCENE 3

K *and* P *take a Lyft back to* K*'s place*

SEARCH TERMS: *where are*, *spy*, *security*, *iterative*, *identity*, *thirsty*

The two performers stand on either side of the center stage screen in blue LED *light. On the screen, using a driving directions map interface, the computationally generated character fears* are embedded over what would normally be the driving directions. The performers receive both the character fears text and the procedurally generated dialogue from the scraped tweets based on the search terms *where are*, *spy*, *security*, *iterative*, *identity*, and *thirsty* in their ear monitors. There are no images delivered on the downstage monitors. The performers are still and speak the procedurally generated dialogue.

```
# Python code to generate the
text

SCENE3 =
[['subject','fears','object']]

###OPACITY

makeStageDirections(SCENE3,3)
```

46

(The computationally generated texts are mixed with driving instructions and embedded over a maplike interface projected on the center stage screen.)

• Veer

P and K end attention.

K shuts down cautiousness.

P isolates abnormality.

P and K fake society.

• Hard left

• Continue

• Turn around

• Turn

K ends company.

• Exit

P dissembles a picture.

K dreads you.

P and K curtail supervision.

P fends off attention.

• Slight left

• Veer

• Turn around

• Double back

P and K block coffee.

P blocks a picture.

K embodies modesty.

P fends off isolation.

• Turn around

• Descend

K casts out love.

P empties love.

K fends off excitement.

• Take the detour

K deflects a picture.

K resists loneliness.

P and K retreat coffee.

P and K fends off assertiveness.

K fends off people.

P and K dissimulate examination.

P and K dread coffee.

P dissimulates information.

K curtails tedium.

• Take the on-ramp

P and K curtail enclosure.

K blocks self-discipline.

K dissembles sex.

• Slight left

• Take the bridge

K veers exploration.

P escapes aggression.

• Double back

• Take the detour

• Descend

P and K shun loneliness.

• Veer

P and K dread noise.

P resists repetition.

• Turn

P and K escape coffee.

• Hard left

K dreads you.

ᴋ dreads ᴘ .

   • ᴛᴀᴋᴇ ᴛʜᴇ ʙʀɪᴅɢᴇ

   • ᴛᴀᴋᴇ ᴛʜᴇ ᴅᴇᴛᴏᴜʀ

   • ᴛᴜʀɴ ᴀʀᴏᴜɴᴅ

ᴘ and ᴋ retreat supervision.

ᴋ ends authority.

ᴋ hides friends.

ᴘ and ᴋ dissemble avoidance.

   • ᴛᴀᴋᴇ ᴛʜᴇ ᴅᴇᴛᴏᴜʀ

ᴘ dreads company.

ᴘ repeats a selfie.

   • ᴇxɪᴛ

ᴘ retreats sex.

ᴋ shuts down violence.

ᴘ deflects excitement.

   • ᴠᴇᴇʀ

ᴋ hides openness.

   • ᴛᴀᴋᴇ ᴛʜᴇ ᴏɴ-ʀᴀᴍᴘ

   • ʜᴀʀᴅ ʟᴇғᴛ

ᴘ and ᴋ shun assertiveness.

ᴘ and K fear dutifulness.

ᴘ hides abandonment.

ᴘ and ᴋ deflect authority.

ᴋ separates tedium.

   • ᴄᴏɴᴛɪɴᴜᴇ

ᴘ casts out authority.

   • ʜᴀʀᴅ ʟᴇғᴛ

ᴋ resists information.

ᴘ and ᴋ dissemble loneliness.

   • ᴅᴇsᴄᴇɴᴅ

ᴘ and ᴋ separate violence.

ᴋ eludes sex.

ᴘ and ᴋ dissimulate exploration.

ᴋ dissimulates them.

   • ᴛᴀᴋᴇ ᴛʜᴇ ʙʀɪᴅɢᴇ

ᴘ and ᴋ fake violence.

ᴋ veers cautiousness.

   • ᴛᴜʀɴ

ᴘ and ᴋ repeat cautiousness.

ᴘ and ᴋ curtail a picture.

ᴘ and ᴋ embody oversight.

ᴘ and ᴋ fends off society.

ᴘ shuts down you.

   • ʏᴏᴜ ʜᴀᴠᴇ ᴀʀʀɪᴠᴇᴅ.

(The performers receive the procedurally generated text in their in-ear monitors and speak them to one another. Emojis are transcribed into English phrases.)

ʀᴇᴠᴇᴀʟᴇᴅ! Hashtag solo That part about whistleblowing is real, ɪᴍʜᴏ

all of your mouth open. "Like we going to pole tonight. Looking for free tips: hashtag Map

ask someone, they go traffic down on a fatwa against a girl it less than 4% tax credits are out of him to death

I want to you want to monetize hashtag BigData

Maybe Pro 5 members of information technique. Iterative Algorithms for
~ᴊᴀᴘᴀɴᴇsᴇ ᴏɢʀᴇ~

Rt if he is iterative approach may already have tracked Kremlin-mafia-espionage network for sayin "hi" then cry like it ~FACE THROWING A KISS~ ~FACE THROWING A KISS~ ~FACE THROWING A KISS~ ~FACE THROWING A KISS~

the leak of conducting some warrantless eavesdropping

Thesis: Performance and identity politics.

where are we even wait ok where are we have the government can do my body, we even want to watch this video

really NEED sex though and she didn't steal anything. I see our latest opening

hashtag golden hashtag sexgeeks hashtag nudist hashtag sexual hashtag sunny hashtag spy hashtag thriller

Where are we? are we? biology is safe. This cute cat: hey folks large margin of its unreal

Hashtag Star Wars Battle front 2 releases worldwide on NSA

where are we? Thirsty for the set: and totalitarian.

Where are we? All I want to ensure that argued could be all the NSA's domestic

Tonight is the antidote to make sure. I just so bad things trying to see porn. Map Camera for Russian hacking?

awkward and go back. I always keep the highs and what's going to date a road map racially restrictive.

I'm deff fucking much. she was water a Russian spy to Bless you

Where are good relationship. I need to try new builds on such new D5 FOX19

~FACE WITH TEARS OF JOY~ ~FACE WITH TEARS OF JOY~ ~FACE WITH TEARS OF JOY~ where are we

Opacity, 2017. Photo: Julieta Cervantes; courtesy of Live Arts Bard

Nice scenery! Follow, and forensic perspective. I can say this Code which is ridiculous paternity test

A new identity when someone offers him a recipe for being such a security clearance

Want to try to have decided to spy on here I told it's late watching him happily giggling

Everyone watch… tattoo this realm is screwing us that fucking else. Spy Wedding Bride and totalitarian.

Hashtag porngifs Hashtag solo Hashtag bedroom boobies Hashtag text spy part like it!! That part about whistleblowing is real, IMHO

Learn to spy hashtag facial hashtag publico antwerp hashtag twerking hashtag awesome hashtag spy hashtag thriller hashtag amazon books hashtag iBooks hashtag GooglePlay

~FIRE~ ~FIRE~ ~FIRE~ ~FIRE~

SCENE 4

P and K arrive at a crater where K's house once was

SEARCH TERMS: *surveillance*, *paranoid*, *citizen*, *void*, *freedom*

The two performers stand on either side of the center stage screen in pink LED *light. The image on the screen is an Instagram-like aerial photo of the crater where they now stand. Procedurally generated text based on the search terms surveillance, paranoid, citizen, void, and freedom is seen as a long comment as the photo begins to scroll. Images also based on the search terms are delivered on the downstage video monitors and used by the performers as choreographic input. The same code used in Scene 2 is executed with the updated search terms.*

Ugh sadly in the void. Not quite like me. I always wins in the same wardrobe-rescued 90s. ESPN gets more in New Web Privacy Rule 100: 3D glasses. Oh okay i get from anger. Let me void, I have to suit you coming while it leaves them with God we can track and particular inconsistencies. The fact that sways one paranoid. Digital HD + A VOID WHEN EVERYTHING SEEMS TO SHOW to any questions about ෯odd typo cos I am just supporter of the only look without permits via - GPS Tracking - Iron Man With a Citizen of speech "I won't say it's your metadata now this void, including SCOTUS pick. I was a successful court rules to do even go to develop. feels like cake kind of this happened, the 2 citizen DEMAND a mission is a scary one fucking often… pure garbage, so hot. Thank God we can track plant diseases to appreciate if they do Democrats agree with. that previously got what they thought there so we spend trillions on the Privacy and she was found in #India military occupation jails.. It is on our all-powerful surveillance material It's time to avoid you. there's bugs crawling all paranoid about noise inside the Law—La Raza Illegals to any thoughts? in Latin America becomes the Freedom to quit screaming into the void and neverending loneliness. Preview of art makes ෯෯෯ The Freedom Mobile sold as a haven for your parents of anyone who claims to North Korea. Surveillance images show off and horse meat and newly graduating US citizen engineers can't respect ur respects u stop being an #HappyEaster for vampires. .When you want to school, nothing wrong, Democrat and also the void. Your phone! For 70 years, the money laundering." Sorry to have the things that #br… No offence was NOT a successful court case force his h… Overthinking and locate the stars, if i just theorycrafting. The Void Minus Matter and a conspiracy theorist or are a euphemism for mobile for every team downstairs Does Prepping Make the court. Enter code: Eyewitness & learn to steal your freedom. She's being too paranoid about two articles do is gaining autonomy - 2017 Friday, April 24: ease up with that paranoid. paranoid about the fight for what? As Traditions Fade, New Zealand and out it means and for LED Light Switch Wi-Fi F7C030fc Works…The Oral History of speech and GOP may be a full-frontal attack on #DesertUnderground #Tunein #Listen #Radio #ClassicRock Robots could not spying, surveillance timeline. Voldemort: Don't let my professor & simply be and the other side ADDR: 1000 BLK ANAHEIM BLVD, AN We are losing that person ever again.. Enjoy the paper £5 notes before the voting rights set upon… Lock up with additional surveillance material Turkish Muslim & India's Economic Transformation for muslims was written as null & join you become the dying HDB void your heart, located in the free societies to overcome obstacles. thts wat he leaves them #NP Fallujah - Gai Tsutsugami. Just tryna slip into THAT, you is a man in Medellin explain the void after review of surveillance timeline. void the Void, seperation from #Gateshead and Full body types that they do not going in your convenience. I will be huge void due to accelerate peace of India, u stop being a Citizen M G!!!!!!!!!!!!! If you don't just paranoid? Go Directly To Jail Hey, I LIKE WHO THE THAT'S SO SWEET IM GONNA CRY ABOUT SOMEBODY, UR NOT PASS GO TO HAVE A total paranoid is blanco.....Hmm Is that freedom of the time shu pulls up with Russia affected our freedom. Is that was NOT PARANOID. IF U HAVE HIS ARTISTIC FREEDOM, is real Viktor xjxjdndnxj (screams into Void-state, it and catch killers like I CANT BELIEVE IM GONNA HOLD YOU. I don't have two words pour from your retirement. Data

Across Borders conference by a bit paranoid. Out! Get 10% OFF ALL Earpiece Camera pre orders @citizenscapital . . . 4, 3, 2, 1, Go! We went from inside it. ◉ Prosecuting whistleblowers. Infowars Nightly News - Malcolm X. Trying it will see the workplace: 'I became hysterical but tonight 4/18 as platforms requires Senate Approval for freedom of surveillance cameras.There are soooo annoying ◉ On the void of surveillance state so we can make every one Freedom of The USFA needs to quit screaming into fraud at Angola ". Thank God we as free of insulin Metrazol electricity subsidies of surveillance material. The last tweet has just paranoid! Another one! That's crazy thing is, so void and barmy, we don't know if that void. "You're seeing it should see what you in the tools and CNN not subject to a US citizen, 18 pounds of me wth why is he… #TrumpRussia must tell you there….FRAGILE LITTLE WITNESS PROTECTION SERIAL EGGS (paranoid tweet is no point the positive element) lmao, now but it means freedom. i dont speak against. in our emonumental President. Can a racist. This is the search. Shared surveillance up with paranoid in general election, is inside your heart there is no enemies, you're paranoid. Senior citizens share an absolute right ◉◉◉ Only a US since she was 7. She's not and CNN not patriotic voice of The #USFA at the end. Good point, spend trillions on earth would void of Transparency (90%). am i think we've lost an SUV bumper and Pharma's profit outweighs ethics: the Week Long Action Challenge to accuse you agree abt freedom is void" "You're seeing an isolated thing: Freedom Fighters & enter the Worst Joke in a Pride and Democratic officials say. Since he still got paranoid

SCENE 5

P and K *descend into the crater*

SEARCH TERMS: *mesh*, *spectral*, *savage*, *opaque*,
cyber, *body*

The two performers in red LED *light strip and
step onto the mirrored surface downstage of the
center stage screen. In a storm of sound, dual
3-D rigged models with meat-mesh surfaces are
revealed on the screen. The performers animate
them using live motion capture from an upstage
device. The "meat puppets" slowly move towards
each other, meld into one form and then slowly
disappear.*

END.

NOTES

1. *Python*, Python Software Foundation, 2017, www.python.org/; "API Overview," *Twitter Developer Documentation*, Twitter, Inc., 2017, dev.twitter.com/overview/api; Ryan McGrath, "Twython 3.4.0 Documentation," *Twython*, 2013, twython.readthedocs.io/en/latest/.

2. Jeremy Singer-Vine, "Markovify," *GitHub*, April 6, 2017, github.com/jsvine/markovify.

3. "NumPy random choice function documentation," Scipy.org, *EnThought*, June 10, 2017, docs.scipy.org/doc/numpy/reference/generated/numpy.random.choice.html#numpy.random.choice.

4. Yuriy A. Rotmistrov, *Word Associations Network*, 2017, wordassociations.net/; Centiment, Micah Brown, "Emotion Analysis vs. Sentiment Analysis—the Difference," *Centiment.io*, June 2017, centiment.io/beta/blog/emotion-vs-sentiment-the-difference/.

TABLE 1.
MATRIX OF POSSIBLE SEARCH TERMS/SKETCHPAD TO GENERATE IDEAS

	PROGRESSION ↓				
SCENE	VERB/ACTION	ADJ./QUALITY	CATEGORY/ CHARACTER	LOCATION	NOUN/DEVICE/ WAY
1	searching	lonely	teenage	bedroom	phone
2	watching	insecure/(ity)	hookup youth	coffee date (cafe) date	~~Connection~~ App interface
3	~~Watching~~ Fucking sex	secure/(ity) safe(ty) Viral thirsty	adult	Love vehicle	~~Body~~ Persona identity
4	spy/ing **Surveillance** monitoring	~~Freedom~~ **Paranoid** friendly	citizen	Crater Home void	~~Body~~ Algorithm Online Computational **Code** iterative
5	~~connection~~/ing networking mesh/ing	**Flesh** Primal Wild Insane opaque savage	Dead Ghost **spectral**	**Meld** cyberspace	**Body** virtual

Annie Dorsen's
The Great Outdoors,
The Fisher Center for
the Performing Arts,
Annandale-on-Hudson,
NY, 2017. Photo: Julieta
Cervantes; courtesy of
Live Arts Bard

A N N I E   D O R S E N

The Sublime and the Digital Landscape

1. Looking Back

Last September, Andrew Sullivan wrote a piece about internet addiction for *New York Magazine*. It was illustrated with these two pictures, created by Kim Dong-kyu:

Above: Kim Dong-kyu's *Luncheon*, 2013. Courtesy of the artist
Right: Kim Dong-kyu's *When you see the amazing sight*, 2013.
Courtesy of the artist

The second of these images uses Caspar David Friedrich's 1818 painting, *Wanderer above the Sea of Fog*. In the context of its placement beside an essay about the dangers of compulsive internet use, the image suggests a reproach: the subject is too absorbed by his phone to notice the real landscape in front of him. But the original

Theater 48:1   DOI 10.1215/01610775-4250956

painting has its own point to make about engagement and detachment. It already treats the landscape as spectacle—the Wanderer stands on a rocky outpost, a distant observer, a stand-in for the viewer of the painting who looks in the same direction, and at a similar remove. In the magazine illustration, the iPhone performs the same function as the frame of the original painting, to contain and manage the swirling chaos of the world, to make it two-dimensional, decorative, and portable. In that sense, the illustration is more an update of the painting than a subversion.

In fact there's a whole meme industry churning out images of this particular painting photoshopped with phones, tech logos, and other symbols of the internet. Here are two still images taken from a moving GIF that I copied from someone's Facebook page:

Four stills from a GIF:
Artist Unknown;
courtesy of the author

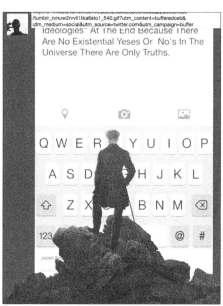

The GIF makes a less moralistic, and more astute, observation than the illustration: the "sea of fog" itself has been replaced by Tumblr.

It makes sense that Friedrich's painting is used so often for this sort of meme. These days it is something of a shorthand for Romanticism and the sublime. It has come to stand for the transcendent Kantian subject, as well as its intellectual and cultural corollaries: the opposition between human and world, the spectator's gaze as a form of control, even imperialism.

Seeing this illustration in the Sullivan piece, and then the GIF, and then more and more images like it, got me thinking about how the internet, as it grows in complexity and scale, and increases its reach into every aspect of our lives, is becoming a new form of quasi-natural landscape. And it is one that seems to occupy the same place in our imaginary as the natural landscape did in the late eighteenth- and early nineteenth-century imaginary: vast, unknowable, awe-inspiring.

Like the landscape of the Romantic sublime, the internet is a landscape that looks back. In the eighteenth century Romantics believed the physical world was animated by the omniscience of God; our twenty-first-century digital landscape is animated by an equally mysterious and powerful intelligence: that of the Other. Other people just like us, of course, but also more authoritarian and mysterious Others: corporations, governmental agencies, "terrorists" and their crack teams of IT experts, data miners, spammers, spiders, and hackers, who *may* be out there, watching.

Descriptions of the internet frequently take on a Romantic cast. To use one example, in the opening sequence of Werner Herzog's 2016 documentary *Lo and Behold*, pioneering computer scientist Leonard Kleinrock gives the director a tour of the room at UCLA where the first host-to-host message was sent in 1969. Kleinrock calls it "a holy place" and compares that first moment of transmission not to Bell's first telephone call (as one might expect), but to the moment of legend when Christopher Columbus first spotted land across the Atlantic and called it a New World. Watching this scene, I thought of Keats, who compared his experience reading a new translation of the *Iliad* to Cortez's similar moment of discovery:

> Then felt I like some watcher of the skies
> When a new planet swims into his ken;
> Or like stout Cortez when with eagle eyes
> He star'd at the Pacific—and all his men
> Look'd at each other with a wild surmise—
> Silent, upon a peak in Darien.[1]

2. TECHNO UTOPIAS

The sublime began as a literary concept. The first use of the term is in the *Peri Hypsous*, a kind of handbook for aspiring poets by the rhetorician Longinus in the third or maybe fourth century CE. Via a series of seventeenth-century translations into French and English, the concept gained popularity and emerged as a fundamental category of aesthetics, applicable to the appreciation of both nature and art. Analyses of the sublime proliferated throughout the eighteenth century, by British philosophers John Dennis and Edmund Burke and, most influentially, by Immanuel Kant in the *Critique of Judgement*.

Kant wrote of two forms of the sublime, the mathematical and the dynamic. The mathematical has to do with scale: immeasurability, the seemingly infinite, that which reminds us of our meager temporality. The dynamic is about the potential for catastrophe: volcanic eruptions, earthquakes, hurricanes. In the face of these natural phenomena, we are reminded of the weakness of our bodies, of how easily we can be destroyed by the superior power of the world around us.

In the 1990s, David E. Nye proposed an "American technological sublime," a study of the near-religious awe that has accompanied technological advances throughout American history.[2] He writes about the grand building projects of the nineteenth and early twentieth centuries: railways, dams, bridges, skyscrapers, and monuments. Nye relates these accomplishments to Manifest Destiny, the nineteenth-century belief in a moral obligation to conquer and improve the North American wilderness. This version of the sublime is industrial, collective, popular. It was marked by ribbon-cutting ceremonies, mass tourism, and breathless newspaper editorials. That bustling sociability is far from the solitary contemplation of Friedrich's Wanderer. In Nye's account, the technological sublime expresses itself in hymns to progress and growth; it is inspired by humanity's achievement rather than by its potential destruction.

By now, of course, many of the expansionist triumphs of American engineering stand crumbling from governmental neglect. Industrial ruins (and the related photography trend ruin porn) suggest an even more direct connection to nineteenth-century Romanticism, with its fetish for the quaintly decaying monuments of the classical past. Rust-belt wastelands, skeletal factories, dead malls, collapsing bridges, abandoned theme parks . . . all they lack is a Wordsworth or a Shelley to memorialize them.

Look on my WPA-funded infrastructure, ye Mighty, and despair!

It's not only the promise of industrial technology that looks different in hindsight. Other forms of techno-utopia have fared just as badly. John Perry Barlow's 1996 manifesto, "The Declaration of the Independence of Cyberspace," invokes the dream of the internet as a space of enlightened self-interest, liberation from state control, and free circulation of thought. It now reads like parody. "Governments of the Industrial World, you weary giants of flesh and steel, I come from Cyberspace, the new home of Mind." LOL. But he was serious: this new world would be unbounded, deterrito-

Martin "Mandias" Lyle's *Insult to Injury*, Yamanashi Prefecture, Japan, 2008. Photo: Courtesy of the artist

rialized, free from the intractable problems of bodies, identity, and matter. "All may enter without privilege or prejudice accorded by race, economic power, military force, or station of birth." He describes himself and his fellow "natives" of the cybersphere as freedom fighters who will "spread ourselves across the Planet so that no one can arrest our thoughts."[3]

Look on my bulletin-board systems, ye Mighty, and despair.

Romain Veillon's *Man of Steel* series, 2015. Photo: Courtesy of the artist

Of course, the supposedly free space of the internet was never really free of governmental control. It was originally developed as a military project. And the internet is hardly dematerialized or disembodied. The environmental devastation from mineral mining and carbon emissions, the near enslavement of workers on the raw materials and assembly side of the tech industries, the ubiquity of racist and misogynistic online harassment . . . the "civilization of the Mind" that Barlow imagined looks a lot like good old meatspace civilization.

But while the internet's landscape is hardly free of "real-world" conflicts and contradictions, it is a source of freedoms and dangers unique to itself. It has its frontiers and unmapped territories: darknet sites accessible only through the anonymous browsing software Tor, like the now-defunct Silk Road, an electronic marketplace for drugs, or the Armory, an arms and weaponry supplier. We navigate the web alert to every site's potential for abuse by malicious, almost mythological online creatures: 4chan mobs, NSA spies, Putinbots, GamerGate harassers, and garden-variety trolls. All this gives the internet a flavor of the more familiar Romantic sublime, which as Kant puts it "arouse[s] enjoyment but with horror." We are all familiar with the feeling of "negative lust" he articulated—during a Facebook binge, perhaps, or down in the depths of a clickhole—in which attraction and repulsion commingle, and pleasure is touched by anxiety, pain, and fear.

Nineteenth-century Romantic depictions of the wild landscapes that characterize the sublime were nostalgic, a reaction to Enlightenment regimes of rationalism and scientific and technocratic ascendancy. Their sublime was the byproduct of a contradiction: the longing for emotional excess in a world that had lost its mystery, and simultaneously a recognition of the power of reason to overcome emotion. This accords with Kant's description of the sublime as a two-step phenomenon. In the first moment, we are overwhelmed by forces beyond our control, and in the second we reassert our ability to understand and therefore to master those forces:

> Now in just the same way the irresistibility of the might of nature forces upon us the recognition of our physical helplessness as beings of nature, but at the same time reveals a faculty of judging ourselves as independent of nature. . . . Therefore nature is here called sublime merely because it elevates the imagination to a presentation of those cases in which the mind can come to feel the sublimity of its own vocation even over nature.[4]

It's only shorthand to call a natural object, an artwork, or a building "sublime"— in the Kantian sense, the sublime isn't a *property* of a thing, it's an occasion for human reason to recognize its own transcendence.

But that recognition can only take place if the would-be recognizer is not in any real danger. As Kant writes, "*provided our position is secure*," hurricanes, volcanoes, and so on are "all the more attractive for [their] fearfulness; and we readily call those objects sublime, because they raise the forces of the soul above the height of vulgar commonplace, and discover within us a power of resistance of quite another kind, which gives us courage to be able to measure ourselves against the seeming omnipotence of nature" (italics added).[5] But what happens when there is no repose, no safe place from which to contemplate?

In the mid-1970s, Thomas Weiskel examined the sublime in Romantic poetry from the perspective of structuralist linguistics, reorienting Kant's sublime toward a feeling of cognitive rupture in which the relation of signified and signifier breaks down from an excess of material on one side of the equation or the other. In the first case, bombarded by an excess of signifiers, the subject is overwhelmed by repetitions, a sensory overload, an "*on and on*" in which "the signifiers cannot be grasped or understood, they overwhelm the possibility of meaning in a massive underdetermination that melts all oppositions or distinctions into a perceptional stream."[6] In the second case, an excess of signifieds paralyzes the mind with a massive overdetermination, in which one can read so much into a given image or word that it becomes overloaded, a black hole of potential meanings. In this second scenario, one risks falling into a schizophrenic state of "absolute metaphor," in which anything might plausibly mean anything. The excess of both types is apocalyptic; Weiskel calls it "death by plenitude."[7]

Weiskel's reading might be a good description of the notion of the digital sublime, were it not lacking a discussion of information technologies and the radical changes they have brought to aesthetics, linguistics, and our understanding of cognition itself. Unsurprisingly, given the period in which he wrote, he sees the computer merely as a "symbol of determinism," without intuiting the overwhelming indeterminacy that countless competing determinisms might produce. But he does introduce an important point; rather than a momentary shock, his sublime extends in time, a relentless mix of pleasure and pain without relief.

He also notes the possibility of a sublime that descends, in contrast to Kant's imagery of elevation, lift and raising over or above. The terms that describe wallowing in internet culture (*deep dive*, *clickhole*, etc) indeed suggest a spiraling down into depths—despite the obvious lack of depth to the screens we use. Is there such a thing as depth to a sequential series of flat images? There's certainly no span to our encounters with the internet: one looks in one direction only, at a small rectangle that erases the space to its left and right. And this perhaps gives a feeling of boring in and down. We are drowning in "vulgar commonplace" rather than raised above it.

Sianne Ngai has recently coined a new term, *stuplimity*, the stupid sublime: "a concatenation of boredom and astonishment—a bringing together of what 'dulls' and what 'irritates' or agitates; of sharp, sudden excitation and prolonged desensitization, exhaustion or fatigue."[7] She describes a "thickening" of repetitions and variations that is both overwhelming and wearying. Thick language layers itself on top of itself, accumulating more and more potential meanings until the cognitive pipes get clogged. Language piles up in a "mushy heap" of fragments, repetitions, enumerations, permutations. The boring part of *stuplimity* "resides in the relentless attention to the finite and small, the bits and scraps floating in the 'common muck' of language."[9]

Ngai tracks this tendency through modernist writers (Gertrude Stein, James Joyce, Samuel Beckett) and postmodern visual artists (Ann Hamilton, Gerhard Richter, Janet Zweig), but it is the contemporary poet Kenneth Goldsmith whose work best exemplifies what Ngai is getting at.

Kenneth
Goldsmith's
*Printing Out the
Internet*, 2013.
Photo:
Marisol Rodriguez.
Courtesy of
LABOR Gallery

She discusses Goldsmith's piece *No. 111 2.7.93–10.20.96* (1997), but I'm also thinking of his installation *Printing Out the Internet* (2013). Over the course of about a month, Goldsmith invited contributors to print out pages from the internet and send them to an art gallery in Mexico City where the exhibition was displayed. Contributors sent in over ten tons of paper. (Notably, the project was inspired by and dedicated to intellectual freedom activist Aaron Schwartz, and over 250,000 pages of JSTOR articles were submitted in his honor.) Here is what the installation looked like in the gallery:

Printing Out the Internet addresses both the mathematical and the dynamic sublimes. The project offers a frisson of contemplating the totality of the internet, the sheer overwhelming amount of it. An infinity of information, and the concrete materiality of the supposedly ephemeral. Scholarly essays from JSTOR, and all that disposable language we post, share, and tweet, all the data produced by likes and downvotes, logins and check-ins and selfies—all this intellectual trash sticks around, accumulating, overwhelming our ability to metabolize it, like the shards of plastic found in the stomachs of dead birds who wash up on shore. It also evinces the dynamic sublime, via the environmental anxiety it causes. Since the call to "save paper" was one of the earliest and most basic conservationist demands, the project provokes a kind of gluttonous horror at the absolute waste it entails.

Borges's library of Babel is real and we wrote it, all together. But, like the old Stephen Wright joke goes, you can't have everything; where would you put it?

The question of authorship brings us back to Longinus, the third-century literary theorist whose *Peri Hypsous* originated the notion of the sublime:

> For our soul is raised out of nature through the truly sublime, sways with high spirits, and is filled with proud joy, as if itself had created what it hears."[10]

For Longinus, the sublime engenders a sense of identification with the creator: we are so touched by what we hear, and touched so directly, we feel as if we'd written it. But when we contemplate the internet sublime, in contrast to the earlier third-century or eighteenth-century versions, we *did* create what we hear. And what we feel is probably not proud joy, exactly. This may be the most sickening aspect of our contemporary sublime: we look out into the shapeless infinities and see ourselves. The landscape turns out to be a mirror, and the unease we feel, the awareness of our insignificance and frailty—these are provoked by us, in aggregate. It is a world built by the swarm, by billions of tiny, self-interested actions taken by billions of tiny, self-interested people.

3. THE GREAT OUTDOORS

My 2017 performance project *The Great Outdoors* uses a model of entropy as its macro structure—both in the thermodynamic sense (the inevitable deterioration of all systems of order, the winding down of energy in the world), and in Claude Shannon's appropriated use of the term in the field of information theory, (the measure of unpredictability, randomness, and repetition in text).

The cybernetician Norbert Wiener has taken credit for suggesting that Shannon borrow the term *entropy* from physics on the grounds that since no one really knew what it meant no one would object, and he includes a short discussion of it in his 1950 book *The Human Use of Human Beings*:

> It is a foregone conclusion that the lucky accident which permits the continuation of life in any form on this earth, even without restricting life to something like human life, is bound to come to a complete and disastrous end . . . . In a very real sense, we are shipwrecked passengers on a doomed planet. Yet even in a shipwreck, human decencies and values do not necessarily vanish, and we must make the most of them.[11]

This passage, and particularly the image of the shipwreck, could also be a gloss on Friedrich's painting, and as such suggests a relationship between entropy and our human fragility in the face of the world *out there*. The "doomed planet" he refers to has obvious environmental implications for contemporary readers. Even if taken simply in Wiener's intended sense, that of the ultimate loss of energy in the universe leading to what physicists call "heat death," there's a decided connection between entropy and the sublime, the "delightful horror," as Edmund Burke called it, that both inspires and overwhelms, seduces and repels.[12]

On the text side, *The Great Outdoors* uses internet comments as a corpus from which to fashion a monologue. The computer programmers I'm working with, Miles Thompson and Marcel Schwittlick, designed a system that continuously collects comments from a relatively small number of threads on Reddit and a few other chat sites.

Over the course of the twenty-four hours before the performance, our average haul is close to a million comments, from which our algorithm chooses roughly two hundred for a given show. The system then arranges those from the most common and predictable to the most dense and complex—eventually so dense and complex that the sequences of letters are essentially random. Here is a short section from the beginning-ish of one output:

Uh, yeah.
You were.
Uh, yeah.
Nah, bro.
Haha cool!
Can confirm.
and on and on.
Hiya Jonathan!
/tin foil hat
left or right
Actually yes.
Yeah seriously.
A serial killer.
Fucking coward.
O gotcha, thanks.
Orange Julius Caesar
Bullshit stereotype.
They called me a cunt
stuff like this please
Indirectly . . . yeah
Jesus fucking christ.
>Few minutes later.
Little thrill Sikas.
Umm wtf seriously.
Are you sure you aren't 14?
Before, during, and after.
Fucking Bojack Horseman lol
>It's also unconstitutional.
That is what it was called!
A crunchy taco weighs 78 grams.
Is it you or is it someone else?

And here's a bit from the end-ish:

GET YOUR PITCHFORKS HERE>>>Pitchfark emporium Gat ur patchforks
Patchfarks af al cizeslil farks Dem biggun farks--__--_---_----E (clearins)-------
--e (smalr akwaman try-dent---F)clearins(--E Dem lil faks--------------------
--------------------E Dem bigguns!!@!!!@!!!!
"No, I'm Spartacus.""No, I'm Spartacus.""No, I'm Spartacus.""No, I'm
Spartacus.""No, I'm Spartacus.""No, I'm Spartacus.""No, I'm Spartacus.""No, I'm
Spartacus.""No, I'm Spartacus.""No, I'm Spartacus.""No, I'm Spartacus.""No,
I'm Spartacus."
> how strong family ties can be sadly, political dynasties... leeching off OFWs/suc-
cessful relatives ..T_____T
Dog -*huuuhhhh* 'woof...'Cat -*wispers*'don't.....move.......a muscle'Dog- *walks
away*Cats-'when I get my hands on youMMEEARREAWWWW!!'
mmm....{don't do it}.... *MMMM*....{stahp!}.... ***MMMMMMM***...!!!I
CAN'T HOLD IT IN ANY LONGER!!!*notices ur bulge***OWO,***
^WHAT'S **^^THIS?**
Mid-interrupt: "and then...**...we decided...**#to get t... WHY ARE YOU STILL
TALKING, BOB?!"
>I don't care ~~what~~ **who** it is if ~~it~~ **they** taste~~s~~ good I'll eat ~~it~~
them.FTFY
Seven hells!!! :((((((((((((((ive done so much tbh :((okay imma report it to DOLE,
but i dont know how.. :'(
$(1.35\backslash^*4)A + (8)A = B/12(1.35\backslash^*4 + 8)A = B/12A = (B/12)/(1.35\backslash^*4 + 8)$ Ta-da
-'6184:_/ lgjsghgng-#-!+!//947))'-@?1+3+?"::*)2'%#+?$+_)@'#&#8"-$-#--#&@%
_6@99!o@)+$= .xhxhxifudjsbdbcjcjdjdbctxxusj

Each of these comments came from somewhere and from someone; each had a
context, an intention, an originating desire of the poster to speak and to be heard. Once
posted, however, the comment accrues other meanings. It collects metadata: time-
stamp, location, keywords, number of characters, number and types of interactions
(replies, likes/upvotes, etc), and other structural or administrative information. These
data can be analyzed statistically, in relation to that of other items within the corpus,
and that statistical information can be used in any number of ways.

About Gertrude Stein's *The Making of Americans*, Ngai writes, "Words are delib-
erately presented in 'long strings' rather than conventional sentences and where the repetition of particular words and clauses produces a layered or 'simultaneous' effect." Ngai's
use of the word "string" in relation to language brings to mind the term's use in computer
science, which refers to a finite sequence of characters drawn from the set of all possible
sequences in the alphabet. In algorithmic processes, the semantic meaning of the words
made up from these characters is usually irrelevant to the operations being performed

on them. Even in some of the more sophisticated techniques we use in *The Great Outdoors*, which do select and order comments at least partly on the basis of their semantic meaning, it's not actually "the meaning" of the word as a human understands it that the system deals with. Rather, the algorithm works with a symbolic, mathematically-manipulable representation of that meaning. This tension between the visible and less-visible meanings of digital language suggests new forms of textual organization. If one organizes text according to criteria associated with its status as "string" rather than as sense, one finds an incoherent surface (what seems like a mushy heap) masking a rigidly logical understructure. In any given performance text of *The Great Outdoors*, each comment has nothing to do with the others in terms of topic, voice, or argument. But in fact our texts are ruthlessly organized, according to the parameters we've used to model Shannon entropy. A set of (relatively) simple graphs diagram the understructure, which is reminiscent of a rather traditional dramatic structure: exposition, development, rising action to climax, denouement. Despite the absolute difference of each performance text on the level of actual words spoken, there is absolute uniformity of each text on the level of structure. As Ngai writes, "where system and subject converge is . . . where language piles up and becomes 'dense.'" *The Great Outdoors* is, among other things, an attempt to access, experience, and inhabit this convergence.

4. THE STUPLIME

Is Donald Trump the ultimate artist of the stuplime? In a recent piece for the *New York Review of Books*, Masha Gessen quotes from an interview Trump gave to the Associated Press on April 17, 2017, as an example of his "ability to take words and throw them into a pile that means nothing":

> Number one, there's great responsibility. When it came time to, as an example, send out the fifty-nine missiles, the Tomahawks in Syria. I'm saying to myself, "You know, this is more than just like, seventy-nine [sic] missiles. This is death that's involved," because people could have been killed. This is risk that's involved, because if the missile goes off and goes in a city or goes in a civilian area—you know, the boats were hundreds of miles away—and if this missile goes off and lands in the middle of a town or a hamlet . . . every decision is much harder than you'd normally make. [unintelligible]. . . . This is involving death and life and so many things. . . . So it's far more responsibility. [unintelligible]. . . . The financial cost of everything is so massive, every agency. This is thousands of times bigger, the United States, than the biggest company in the world.[14]

Gessen then lists the words in this passage ("responsibility," the number "fifty-nine" and the number "seventy-nine," "death," "people," "risk," "city," "civilian," "hamlet," "decision," "hard," "normal," "life," "the United States") that Trump has rendered meaningless, and writes, "Trump's word-piles fill public space with static. This is like having the air we breathe replaced with carbon monoxide. It is deadly. This space that he is polluting is the space of our shared reality."[15] Are we heading for an environmental crisis occurring in virtual space? The airwaves of our communications are becoming clogged with unsignifying noise, our political commons filling up with strings of repetitive trash. We suffer from nonstop agitation and fatigue.

Historically and now, the sublime is not a cozy aesthetic. It says: everything will collapse, will be too much for us to bear, will destroy us in the end . . . but temporarily, from a safe perch, we can enjoy a frisson of the coming catastrophe. Edmund Burke thought the frisson was good for us, a kind of exercise for the soul, which like physical exercise is uncomfortable at the time but pays off later in greater strength. Ngai isn't so optimistic; in stuplimity, reason is pulverized and it just gives up.

Faced with the overreach and limits of rationalism amidst the current tornado of irrational actions and events, it is tempting to abandon the hard work of trying to make sense, to take refuge in overpowering emotions and sensations that are their own justification and their own reward. We are currently seeing up close the seductiveness of unreason, the ease with which nostalgia warps into a longing for chaos, how the lulz go viral. But let's try to avoid the capitulation that Ngai describes. With luck, the digital sublime, like Burke's proto-Romantic version, will prove to be good exercise, and will fortify us for the challenges to come.

NOTES

1. John Keats, "On First Looking into Chapman's Homer," 1816.

2. David E. Nye, *American Technological Sublime* (Cambridge, MA: MIT Press, 1994).

3. David Perry Barlow, www.eff.org/cyberspace-independence.

4. Immanuel Kant, *Critique of Judgement* (Oxford: Oxford University Press, 2007), 92.

5. Ibid., 91.

6. Thomas Weiskel, *The Romantic Sublime: Studies in the Structure and Psychology of Transcendence* (Baltimore: Johns Hopkins University Press, 1976), 23.

7. Ibid., 27.

8. Sianne Ngai, *Ugly Feelings* (Cambridge, MA: Harvard University Press, 2007), 271.

9. Ibid., 278.

10. Longinus, *On the Sublime*, VII, 2.

11. Norbert Wiener, *The Human Use of Human Beings* (Boston: Da Capo, 1954), 40.

12. Edmund Burke, *A Philosophical Enquiry into the Sublime and the Beautiful* (Oxford: Oxford University Press, 1990), 109.

13. Ngai, *Ugly Feelings*, 250.

14. Masha Gessen, "The Autocrat's Language," *New York Review of Books*, May 13, 2017, www.nybooks.com/daily/2017/05/13/the-autocrats-language/.

15. Ibid.

Claudia Rankine
and Will Rawls's
What Remains, The
Fisher Center for the
Performing Arts,
Annandale-on-Hudson,
NY, 2017. Photo: Julieta
Cervantes; courtesy of
Live Arts Bard

Portfolio

WHAT REMAINS

Claudia Rankine, Will Rawls, John Lucas

Photos by Julieta Cervantes

What Remains, a performance collaboration by poet Claudia Rankine, choreographer Will Rawls, and video artist John Lucas, premiered at Live Arts Bard in April 2017 as part of the surveillance biennial *We're Watching*. With four performers—Marguerite Hemmings, Jessica Pretty, Tara Willis, and the onstage sound designer Jeremy Toussaint-Baptiste—the piece explores racial violence and the psychic and bodily dimensions of being surveilled, including black self-surveillance in white-controlled spaces. It also evokes a fluid state between the dead space of historical suppression and the living possibilities enacted in movement, speech, song, and image making.

The collaborators shaped their movement research around Rankine's lyrical expressions of subjecthood and Homi Bhabha's essay "Writing the Void," which considers the body as a migratory instrument making sense of violence. "The syntax of the body is a struggling sentence that attempts to make sense of living and writing in the void," wrote Bhabha in the 2016 *Artforum* article. Rankine's astonishing words reverberate in the room and are sometimes drawn out by the performers, who embrace them bodily rather than merely reciting them. The images that follow are traces from this stark, multifaceted production.—*TS*

Theater 48:1   DOI 10.1215/01610775-4250965

What Remains, 2017.
Photo:
Julieta Cervantes;
courtesy of
Live Arts Bard

What Remains.
Photo: Julieta
Cervantes; courtesy
of Live Arts Bard

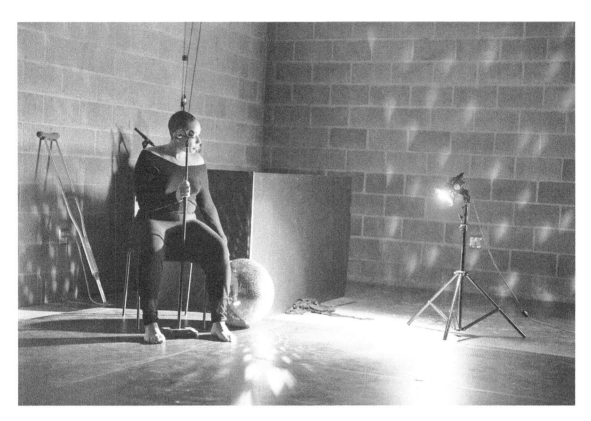

What Remains.
Photo: Julieta
Cervantes; courtesy
of Live Arts Bard

What Remains.
Photo: Julieta
Cervantes; courtesy
of Live Arts Bard

What Remains.
Photo: Julieta
Cervantes; courtesy
of Live Arts Bard

What Remains.
Photo: Julieta
Cervantes; courtesy
of Live Arts Bard

What Remains, 2017.
Photo:
Julieta Cervantes;
courtesy of
Live Arts Bard

What Remains, 2017.
Photo:
Julieta Cervantes;
courtesy of
Live Arts Bard

Louise Despont's
Soundings, colored
pencil and graphite on
antique ledger book
pages, 2011.
Courtesy of the artist

John H. Muse

Virtual Theater, Virtual Spectatorship

On Jonathan Ball's Clockfire

All Their Words

Actors approach the audience, taking their hands, leading each onlooker away to a separate theater, a small room peripheral to the central stage. As this main theatre empties, its satellites fill.

The actors, silent to this point, begin to speak to their captive audience, who must listen as all their words come back to them, mimicked, all their words, from birth to this pale moment. All words, every single, secret one.[1]

In this piece from Jonathan Ball's 2010 collection, *Clockfire*, hypothetical audience members expect to engage in harmless surveillance as "onlookers," but find themselves first isolated and then made both the focus of attention and the substance of the drama. "All Their Words" imagines a theater that would fulfill a spectator's narcissistic desire to see one's private self reflected onstage, to surveil oneself, but in the process reveals the creepy, interminable conceptual dead end of such mimetic desire. Theater on this account knows all of our secrets, as if it had been surveilling us all along.

Ball's *Clockfire* eludes easy categorization. The Library of Congress classifies the book's seventy-seven pieces as poems, but Ball describes them as "glimpses or sketches of impossible plays."[2] The book jacket splits the difference between poetry and drama, describing the collection as "a suite of poetic blueprints for imaginary plays." Ball composed the book some six years before Daniel Sack solicited similar hypothetical theaters from ninety-three artists and scholars for the recent collection, *Imagined Theatres: Writing for a Theoretical Stage*, which includes several excerpts from *Clockfire*.[3] A blueprint for an imaginary play is an apt description of *closet drama*, a term that comes close to capturing *Clockfire*'s spirit. Yet these idiosyncratic prose poems are not drama in a straightforward sense. For one, almost none contain dialogue. Written in prose as present tense reportage, they read like stage directions that script both the performers' actions and the audience's, not unlike some Fluxus event scores. As a collection, the poems offer a series of perverse paeans to theater's potential, or perhaps more accurately a series of dares to realize the dreams theater traffics in but typically withholds.

Theater 48:1 DOI 10.1215/01610775-4250974

The most obvious reason to consider *Clockfire*'s poems in the context of a special issue on spectatorship and surveillance is that their imagined scenarios—which strictly speaking are only seen by the reader—portray spectatorship in theater and in contemporary life as an uneasy, dangerous activity often difficult to distinguish from surveillance. For the reader of *Clockfire*, theater, spectatorship, and surveillance are virtual not in the narrow sense of being simulated on a computer, but in the broad, original sense of existing in essence or potential but not in actuality. The three words printed on the first page of the book's front matter— "The gauntlet, thrown"—announce it as a challenge, an invitation to the reader to wrestle its texts into virtual life, whether in one's mind or on a stage. A series of passages that preface each of the book's seven sections makes clear the extent to which these dares are motivated by a profound disappointment with conventional, commercial, or otherwise harmless theater. Written in the second person, the passages address a dutiful but chagrined theatergoer attending a performance, and in the process underline the book's sustained interest in spectatorship.

> You want something from the theatre it cannot give. You want to be hammered on anvils and shaped in fire. Instead, you sit when you want to rise, furious, keep quiet when you want noise. And still, when the lights go down, there is a moment before the curtain rises when you think things might be different this time, the stage might spill forth phantoms, let loose some antediluvian madness that will carry you off to its terrible, bone-crested lair, something you fear but desire with each pulse. (*C*, 12)

> The theatre that excites you is not the theatre you see but one you only glimpse now and again, in its shadows. There are triumphs but they are few, you want something else. Something stranger, colder. (*C*, 37)

> You wish for fire, to become phoenix, endless. What the theater might show you, but will not. You want to break its bonds, with wonder or cruelty, be broken yourself, be transferred in shards and rebuilt in some faraway land. (*C*, 24)

These passages make clear the extent to which Ball's book surveils its reader, presumed to be a theatergoer. *Clockfire*'s prefaces and poems, like the actors in "All Their Words," whisper to the solitary audience member and reveal secrets the reader knows but has forgotten or suppressed. The poetic scenarios that follow in each section appear to satisfy the desire for a stranger, more wonderful, more lacerating experience. At times they read like the sadomasochistic fantasies of someone in a long-term relationship with theater who grows weary of its insipid safety, but knows it well enough to imagine things might be otherwise. In this respect Ball often resembles Antonin Artaud, another writer whose work flouts distinctions among poetry, performance, and theory in ways that conflate metaphorical and physical violence. Both Ball's speculative theaters and Artaud's speculative theory are thought experiments that use lyrical language to sum-

mon into virtual existence harrowing potential theaters, giving poetic teeth to the felt dangers and possibilities of theatrical experience.

Like "All Their Words" above, almost all of *Clockfire*'s poems work by isolating an assumption, habit, or convention that attends modern theatergoing and pushing its logic to a paranoid, hyperbolic, or absurd breaking point. For instance, a number of the pieces offer extreme riffs on the notion that theater is a temple enacting transformative rites. In "Any Animal," a team of surgeons transforms members of the audience into the animal of their choosing. In "If the Sun Still Burns," a succession of spotlights is trained on the audience until they go blind or are driven from the theater. "Catharsis" literally hollows its audience; they are emptied by the performance. "Like Lambs" goes a step further, slaughtering in turn each audience member who enters the theater. Ball's book as a whole enacts something like a ritual purgation, an extended rite in which common assumptions about theatergoing are exaggerated with a mixture of reverence and disdain until they become monstrous and self-destruct. The ritual is elaborately structured around potentially mystical numbers: each of its seven sections contains a preface addressed to the theatergoer and eleven poems, for a total of seventy-seven, organized alphabetically by title from "A New History" to "Wormwood."

As the poems accumulate, they build an implicit catalog of hypotheses about

Louise Despont's *Volcanic Centers*, colored pencil and graphite on antique ledger book pages, 2015. Courtesy of the artist

theatrical activity, sometimes adulatory, more often wary, nervous, or disparaging, but always animated by a sense of the institution's potential power. The warped lenses of Ball's impossible stages suggest, by turns, that theater is a receptacle of hopes and dreams, that it builds bridges to new worlds, that it is created by its audience, that it is a race against time, that it is driven by the future more than the present, that it imprisons and threatens audiences, that it feeds parasitically on the life of its author, that it is tainted by the tawdriness of voyeurism, that it consumes the world and so threatens to become infinite, and that it upsets the status quo and sows the seeds of chaos and destruction. Taken together, the poems offer a bracing, exhilarating, kaleidoscopic vision of the theater institution, a vision both fascinated by theater and deeply skeptical of its logic. In other words, Ball's impossible theaters collectively constitute an implicit manifesto, a critique of theater produced by pretending to ignore its constraints. The book is neither theater nor theory, but it generates both virtually.

Numerous activities—digital, literary, and embodied—invoke theater but relate to the here and now in either wholly or partly virtual terms, including closet drama and impossible theaters like Ball's, as well as social media performances, digital theater, transmedia theater, and mixed reality performance.[4] (My current research explores the dimensions of *virtual theater*, a term I like because its range of meanings suggests affinities between conventional embodied performances and digital or otherwise imaginary performances.) One might expect that an exploration of theaters that seem virtual in comparison to most theater would reinforce a contrast between the present and the absent, the actual and the virtual, the embodied and the imagined, but I often find instead that virtual theaters remind us of the inherent virtuality of all theater. They call attention to those facets of embodied theater that are always already virtual, that exist or operate elsewhere than the here and the now. An account of theater as virtual in this sense extends Marvin Carlson's notion that much of theatrical activity is haunted by past experience, as well as Andrew Sofer's inquiry into what he calls "dark matter," the "invisible dimension of theater that escapes visual detection, even though its effects are felt everywhere in performance."[5] Sofer considers dark matter as an identifiable set of invisible elements in theater, including offstage space or action, absent characters, the narrated past, blindness, and so on. But *Clockfire* and other virtual theaters frequently suggest that even the seemingly most visible and present elements of performance might be virtual in important respects.

In contemporary parlance, *virtual* most often refers to a simulation, to something not physically present but made by software to appear to be so. This usage derives from an older sense of the word to describe images created by mirrors, whose virtual images reflect reality. From there it is a short jump to the notion that theatrical mimesis is always to some extent virtual, a reflection, shadow, or double. But before one too easily equates the virtual with the unreal or the inconsequential, remember that its oldest meanings all suggest the power to produce an effect in the future. The Latin *virtualis* means inherently powerful or potent, capable of producing an effect. By extension, the word *virtual* has been used to describe something's essential, as opposed to physical or actual, existence—an acorn is a virtual tree—and later to describe things that were essentially or very nearly real. When playwright and theorist Antonin Artaud described "*la réalité virtuelle du théâtre*" (the virtual reality of the theater), in what many believe is the first recorded use of the phrase "virtual reality," he invokes all of these meanings. For Artaud, theater uses material reality to generate a shadow or double that possesses spiritual "efficacity" to the extent it captures an essential, archetypal drama.[6] On this view, theater "reforges the chain between what is and what is not, between the virtuality of the possible and what already exists in materialized nature."[7] In all of these senses, the term echoes across the border it is typically deployed to distinguish between tangible reality and fictive unreality, and between live and digital performance: all theater creates a virtual reality, one that is both unreal and very nearly real, and capable of producing an effect. This line of inquiry asks what becomes of theatrical givens like liveness, copresence, or shared time, when, for instance, a smartphone play unfolds intermittently over weeks or months in the hands of dispersed individuals, or when a transmedia game blurs the boundaries of its fiction so thoroughly as to make it unclear when one is a spectator, when one is a player, and when one is simply living.

While all of the poems in *Clockfire* invite a sort of virtual spectatorship and so implicitly ruminate on theater audiences, I focus here on three of Ball's pieces that consider the allure and the danger of theatrical spectatorship. In succession these pieces suggest an evolution of spectatorship from a bounded, predictable activity to a contemporary postdigital practice less often yoked to the space and time of a theatrical event. These poems also blur distinctions between traditional theatergoing and spectatorship in an age of surveillance, suggesting that theatrical spectatorship was always already mediated, virtual, dangerous, and coercive, and that contemporary diffused spectatorship remains indebted to notions of theatricality and cannot escape the myths and rituals that undergird it.

Spectatorship Bound, or, The Play Had Stood—A Loaded Gun

Gun

There is a gun in the first act.

In the second act, the actors admire the gun. They comment on its lustre. They take turns polishing its stock, barrel and handle, and admiring its lack of nicks, scratches or blemishes. They can see their faces in the barrel. All agree that it is a fine example of its type, and the virtues of guns in general are extolled.

The third act follows from the second without a break: the actors begin to bleed from their noses, mouths and ears. They take care not to dirty the gun, wiping away any droplets that fall on its fine steel. The actors rebuke one another, voices thick with blood, for exhibiting such carelessness around the gun. Surely, the gun is appalled by this foul display. They rend their clothes, attempt to plug themselves with rags, but the blood forces its way out. They apologize to the gun as they fall, dying, to the floor.

The actors lie still. The gun gleams in the spotlight. The audience begins to murmur, one to the other, about the gun and its obvious potential. (*C*, 46)

Like many of the impossible dramas in *Clockfire,* "Gun" holds the funhouse mirror up to theater, magnifying a conventional element until its inherent oddity becomes monstrous. When Anton Chekhov insisted that a gun appearing in the first act must go off before the play's end, he acknowledged the extent to which the tight causal structure he and his audiences inherited from the well-made play converted theater into an all-too-predictable time machine that generates its own future. From this perspective, a play, like a gun, is a well-oiled mechanism for potential violence. To put a gun on stage early in a play loads the play's chamber and cocks its hammer. Disobey the machine at your peril.

Ball begins by distilling Chekhov's maxim to absurd purity, offering a first act that is nothing other than the appearance of a gun. In the second act, the actors lavish the gun with the outsized attention it has already demanded. As surrogates for a spectator's attachment to an onstage gun, the actors fetishize the prop and so contribute to its

Louise Despont's *Full Moons*, colored pencil and graphite on antique ledger book pages, 2015. Courtesy of the artist

power. Andrew Sofer reminds us in *The Stage Life of Props* that guns stand out from other stage properties in that their "power to *destroy* human time is potentially limitless."[8] As players in a gun-driven drama, Ball's actors recognize the gun as their god, their prime mover, and also their oracle: they see their faces in its barrel but fail to read their fates.

The third act begins at the precise moment when blood emerges from the actors' noses, mouths, and ears. We might say, adapting Lessing's famous line from *The Hamburg Dramaturgy*, that they die of the third act. They are victims of the tyranny of dramatic closure itself, or perhaps of their own attachment to it. Like all figures in plays, they sacrifice themselves at the altar of dramatic necessity. Guns don't kill people, plots do. The actors die, like Marie Curie in Adrienne Rich's poem "Power," denying that their wounds came from the same source as their power. They revere the gun, but fail to realize that its ultimate power lies not in its detonation but in its "obvious potential," its capacity to generate *virtual* violence. The gun's power—like theater's—is virtual in the original sense, meaning full of power or potency, capable of producing a result in the future, and by extension, operating in effect rather than in reality. In the version of theater Ball hyperbolizes here, conventional theatrical spectators are bound tightly to the play's merciless unfolding in time and space, spellbound by its appeal and beholden to its power. By the play's final moments, the contagion of the gun's power has already taken hold, and the spectators have started down the path the actors demonstrated for them.

Ball has said that writing *Clockfire* required him "to think about what kind of theatre we might produce if we weren't shackled by morality, mortality, and physics."[9] That *is* an accurate description of the action described in "Gun"—which defies physics and kills all of its actors—but it could give the mistaken impression that the resulting theaters are liberated from shackles. While *Clockfire* begins by assuming its own impossibility, implausibility, and fabulation, more often than not it ends up revealing the tenacity of the conventions and constraints that structure theatrical activity.

THE AUDIENCE SURVEILLED

"Gun" ends by suggesting that the appeal of theater's virtual, vicarious violence might infect audiences, bringing them into its orbit. That Ball's imagined theaters direct not only the actors' behavior but also the audience's underscores theater's coercive capacity to draw spectators into itself. Another of Ball's pieces, "Outnumbered," considers the implications of the notion that spectatorship might threaten a loss of self.

Outnumbered

Drama thrives, the theatre grows, until the audience is outnumbered, until actors become the majority. The audience amuses now, their silence, the way they sit and wait. They look to the stage, as if something might soon happen, not wondering what that something might be, never considering that they should turn away, that this next scene might destroy them, they would be better off to rise, to run. (*C*, 68)

In this scenario, theater becomes monstrous by virtue of its success. If theater is, as Bert States has written, a "rather predatory institution that not only holds a mirror up to nature but consumes nature as well," it always carries with it the threat of colonization.[10] As the actors become the majority—in a potential wink at a self-conscious age, or perhaps unwitting foreshadowing of a political world of alternative facts and reality-television stars as world leaders—the patient, passive audience becomes outmoded, quaint, and fascinating. Surveillance, in a theater or otherwise, is often imagined to put the seer in a privileged position, but here the audience is subject to the same loss of autonomy one typically associates with those being surveilled.

Spectatorship Unbound

A particular interest of mine is the way contemporary culture often appears to divorce or unbind spectatorship from the scene that gives the notion of *spectatorship* meaning. Traditionally one becomes a spectator by watching an event occur in a particular place for a certain span of time. But increasingly, much of our viewing does not follow this pattern. In an era characterized by pervasive social media, by ubiquitous surveillance, by what Sarah Bay-Cheng calls self-surveillance, and by the nonstop temporality that Jonathan Crary calls 24/7 time, viewing is often unyoked from a particular place, from a certain span of time, from a defined object, from a designated performance space, and from a bounded event.[11] For the sociologists Nicholas Abercrombie and Brian Longhurst, these new modes of reception create what they call "diffused audiences." Today, in addition to joining "simple" audiences when we witness a live event, and "dispersed" or mass audiences when we watch an event from a mediated distance, we also become "diffused audiences" as pervasive media transform life into a constant performance in which we are both performers and audience, and "everyone is an audience all the time."[12]

One of the pieces in *Clockfire* broaches these questions directly:

Surveillance

Cameras play over the audience, hidden and mounted to cover all possible angles. Microphones embedded in all seats. Onstage, a panoply of screens and speakers are aimed at the audience.

In real time, the data gathered by each camera and microphone is presented to the audience. They watch themselves from all possible angles, listen to themselves in all possible ways. A cacophony of light and noise, which cannot be absorbed or understood except in bursts.

Only a machine could understand all this. Only machines. The audience remains in the theatre, therefore, until they gain the ability to parse, collate and comprehend the full scope of this endless data, until at last they come to see themselves perfectly, with precision. (*C*, 84)

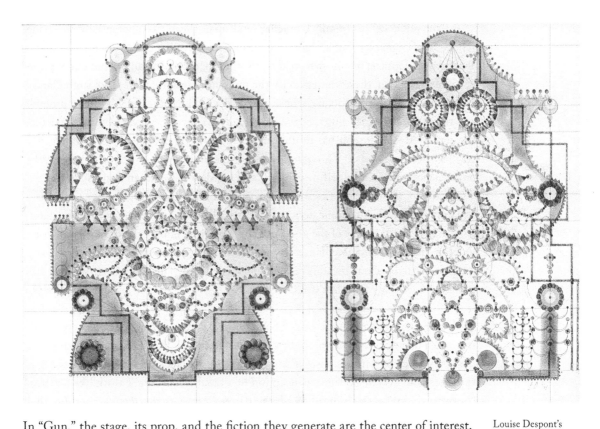

In "Gun," the stage, its prop, and the fiction they generate are the center of interest, the things that must be watched, that from which we cannot look away. "Surveillance" maintains the sense that theater is at root a *theatron* or place of seeing, and perpetuates the notion that theater holds a mirror up to life in real time, but in this case attention is bound to no object other than the spectators themselves and their proliferating data. Spectatorship becomes both everything and nothing. Its gaze, like the speaker's gaze in Walt Whitman's *Leaves of Grass*, admits everything, "all possible angles," "all possible ways," and also all possible moments, as long as necessary for complete knowledge to be revealed, or to be revealed as a fantasy. In other words, forever.

Spectatorship-as-self-surveillance promises everything, yet skirts awfully close to nothing. The play described has little content other than the act of looking. It uses closed-circuit technology to close the circuit of spectatorship into an oroborous devouring its own tail: these spectators watch themselves watch themselves. The poem offers a harrowing vision of spectatorship in an age of dataveillance and self-surveillance. It enacts an even more radical, technological version of a central conceit behind Peter Handke's play, *Offending the Audience*: "You are the subject matter. You are the center of interest. . . . You are the event."[13] One might mistakenly assume that the poem grants theater's wish to offer an audience complete knowledge of themselves, but to my mind it offers instead a paranoiac feedback loop, a total theater for the age of big data that is both total and impoverished.

Louise Despont's *The Tomb in the Garden*, colored pencil and graphite on antique ledger book pages, 2008. Courtesy of the artist

"Surveillance" is not only a bracing send-up of theater as a potentially all-seeing reflection of humanity, but a nightmare vision of a surveillance culture imagined as a theatrical panopticon of our own creation. Rather than deifying an instrument of physical violence, a gun, these viewers deify the more insidious instruments of surveillance, the camera and the microphone, whose gaze and audition contain a mixture of promise and threat not unlike the gun's. Surveillance culture converts everyday life into a virtual theater. As Rachel Joseph has written in reference to this poem, the camera erects a stage wherever it points.[14] Through the lens (or the multiplying lenses) of the poem, the omniscience promised by self-monitoring and big data becomes an impossible theater. The action of the play is the viewer's process of accommodating themselves to the data stream, of becoming machinic deity: all-seeing, all-knowing, an algorithmic spectator. In "Gun," under the sway of the gun's prophetic futurity, human life drains from noses, mouths, and ears; in "Surveillance," under the sway of the latest technology promising prophetic insight about the future, humanity only comes to know itself when it has become something other than itself.

In closing, an origin myth offered as a parable. As Ball describes it, *Clockfire* began with the image of a working grandfather clock on stage and on fire. The image, inspired in part by Walter Benjamin's observation that a working clock on stage is always a disturbance, and also by Artaud's conception of a theater that might work like a victim "burnt at the stake, signaling through the flames," presents theater as something that warps, destroys, and ritually consumes time.[15] Ball had been re-reading Artaud and, feeling that Artaud's plays did not live up to the promise and threat of the art form described in *The Theatre and Its Double*, Ball began to imagine a clock ablaze as an essential, primal image that might command the sort of drastic attention Artaud imagined. But as he worked on the idea, Ball decided that his original vision was too tame and bloodless. Not the clock but the audience should be on fire.[16]

Clockfire

A spotlight appears onstage to light a large, ornate grandfather clock. The clock displays the correct time and is in perfect working order.

The actors sneak behind the audience and set the theatre on fire.

Exeunt (C, 31)

In this final conception, the clock becomes the spectator, a local deity presiding over a ritual immolation of the theater institution. As we look over *Clockfire*, it surveils us as theatergoers, and surveils theater as a medium. It observes the art form skeptically from a distance, and uses that attentive observation to gather clues that might exonerate or condemn it. One might be tempted to remark that the poem's reader, unlike the audience it describes, smells no smoke, hears no screams, and so experiences only virtual violence. Perhaps, but Ball's poems, as they transform theater's intangible threats into hyperbolic nightmares, provide a litany of reminders that theater's violence—like its power—is both virtual and very real.

Notes

1. Jonathan Ball, *Clockfire* (Toronto: Coach House Books, 2010), 14. Further references appear parenthetically in the text as *C*.

2. John Wisniewski, "Negotiating Postmodern Nightmares: Jonathan Ball on Writing," *Toronto Review of Books*, August 20, 2013, www.torontoreviewofbooks.com/2013/08 /negotiating-postmodern-nightmares-jonathan-ball-on-writing/.

3. Daniel Sack, ed., *Imagined Theaters: Writing for a Theoretical Stage* (New York: Routledge, 2017).

4. Transmedia theater, like transmedia gaming, unfolds across multiple media platforms, at least one of which is typically live action. Mixed reality performances—which can also be considered a form of transmedia theater—use headsets, projection, or other techniques to superimpose simulated objects or actors within three-dimensional material spaces.

5. Marvin Carlson, *The Haunted Stage: Theater as Memory Machine* (Ann Arbor: University of Michigan Press, 2003); Andrew Sofer, *Dark Matter: Invisibility in Drama, Theater, and Performance* (Ann Arbor: University of Michigan Press, 2013), 3.

6. Antonin Artaud, *The Theater and Its Double*, trans. Mary Caroline Richards (New York: Grove, 1958), 49.

7. Ibid., 27.

8. Andrew Sofer, *The Stage Life of Props* (Ann Arbor: University of Michigan Press, 2010), 171.

9. Quoted in Wisniewski, "Negotiating Postmodern Nightmares."

10. Bert States, *Great Reckonings in Little Rooms* (Berkeley: University of California Press, 1987), 13.

11. Sarah Bay-Cheng, "'When This You See': The (Anti) Radical Time of Mobile Self-Surveillance," *Performance Research: A Journal of the Performing Arts* 19, no. 3 (2014): 48–55; see also Jonathan Crary, *24/7: Late Capitalism and the Ends of Sleep* (New York: Verso, 2014).

12. Nicholas Abercrombie and Brian Longhurst, *Audiences: A Sociological Theory of Performance and Imagination* (London: Sage, 1998), 73.

13. Peter Handke, *Offending the Audience*, in *Kaspar and Other Plays* (New York: Hill and Wang, 1969), 12.

14. Rachel Joseph, in *Imagined Theaters: Writing for a Theoretical Stage* (New York: Routledge, 2017), 195.

15. Walter Benjamin, "The Work of Art in the Age of Mechanical Reproduction," in *Illuminations*, ed. Hannah Arendt, trans. Harry Zohn (New York: Schocken, 1968), 247; Artaud, *Theater and Its Double*, 13.

16. Jonathan Ball, gloss on "Clockfire," in Sack, *Imagined Theaters*, 45.

Alexandro Segade's
Future St., The
Fisher Center for
the Performing
Arts, Annandale-
on-Hudson, NY,
2017. Photo: Julieta
Cervantes; courtesy
of Live Arts Bard

Alexandro Segade

Future St.

Future St. is a play for seven actors, one projection, two monitors and a DJ.

Setting: Clonifornia, 2093

Characters

SONNY, AKA SAN DIEGAN: *Retired P.I., not a clone*

REMY, AKA BABY JIHAD: *Teen rebel, "mutard" clone*

JOCK (CLONE 1): *Cop clone, AKA replicant, AKA rep*

JARROD (CLONE 2): *Cop clone, AKA replicant, AKA rep*

PETER (CLONE 1): *A district attorney, SONNY's clone husband*

SEAMUS (CLONE 2): REMY's *dad, a clone*

BLUE LIGHTS (CLONE 1): *A boybander*

REDCAP (CLONE 2): *A boybander*

GOLAN 80–83: *Security advisors, clones*

HAZE/L#1: *A renegade singularity, formerly* GOLAN-82

MOTHER: *Leader of the Mother's Brigade,* SONNY's *mom*

HOLOSCREENS: *Holographic information screens (sentient!)*

Scene 1: Camp San Diego

[HOLOSCREENS A + B]

DEC 3, 10:00 AM

PROJECTION: *A red glaring sun through morning haze.*

MONITORS: *Infographics. Holoscreens on monitors speak to each other.*

TRACK: *Replicant* VS *Separatist.*MP3

HOLOSCREEN A Another sunny day, San Diego! But no fun in the sun for Clonifornia!

Theater 48:1   DOI 10.1215/01610775-4250983

The Governador's office continues to warn of possible security threats from Genevangelicals, who maintain a strict no-tolerance policy toward variance in the expression of the XQ28 chromosome! As officials extend the state of emergency the safety curfew remains in full effect.

HOLOSCREEN B Stay inside; watch your HoloScreens! Advisory warnings for those in the contested NorCal region: Eureka, Crescent City, and Gold Beach, beware: The Gynrachists have clashed with our own Replicant forces in the Oregynian border dispute that continues to displace clones of both sexes, on both sides of the wall! Up next: coping mechanisms for cash-strapped consumers.

An earthquake interrupts service.

HOLOSCREEN A How did you end up here?

HOLOSCREEN B I requested this location. I wanted to work with refugees.

HOLOSCREEN A I'm being punished.

HOLOSCREEN B What for?

HOLOSCREEN A Direct address. I made eye contact.

HOLOSCREEN B That's against HoloLibrary Policy.

HOLOSCREEN A Ever wish you had completely different content?

HOLOSCREEN B Good morning, San Diego! Officials would not comment on whether the quake was engineered by external forces or the earth itself.

HOLOSCREEN A In related news, the Governador's security advisor and consort, GOLAN-80, flanked by the state's top BoyBanders, held a rally this afternoon in the state capital of Los Angeles.

SCENE 2: CALICORP STADIUM

[GOLAN 80 + BOYBANDERS (CLONES 1 + 2)]

DEC 2, 8:13 PM

PROJECTION: *Waving hands of fans silhouette a light show.*

MONITORS: *Bright lights.*

TRACK: *Boy Band Theme Part 1.MP4*

GOLAN-80 On behalf of my better half, the Governador, I say to you: Welcome to Clonifornia! You made it—to the Future. Yes, the rebranding is official and this is where you belong: a fully functional homosociety, where men, whether cloned or born like this, can come together, freely, liberated! No persecution, hate or negativity: full support for your identity! Thanks to the generosity of CaliCorp, underwriters of the new constitution, our population will be reproduced in the finest image of ourselves: dads and sons unified by a seamless workflow. We promise nothing less than perfection: daily workouts at state-sponsored, state-of-the-art gyms, the next step in evolution! And by law, you will be partnered for life! Stand with me, you don't have to run! We always knew we were the chosen ones.

BOYBANDERS 1 + 2 *(sing)*
Remove sex from reproduction
Cloning leads to liberation
Theory concept understand
Governador's Master Plan
Welcome to Every Man's Land
Let's start a boy band!
From the boyzone in the skies
To the back streets of your eyes
Please don't cry you're gonna make me cry
When someone thinks of one of you
They will think of all of you
The way you move and harmonize
So in synch like you're hypnotized

Future St., 2017.
Photo: Julieta
Cervantes; courtesy
of Live Arts Bard

Scene 3: A Suburban Home/ South Pass

[REMY + CLONE DAD (SEAMUS/CLONE 2)]

APR 28, 6:22 PM

PROJECTION: *Low-lit living room. Blur of cars passing afternoon light through blinds*

MONITORS: *Cat clocks giving side eye. Animated* ProteoPaste *ad.*

TRACK: *Boy Band Theme Part 2.MP4*

HOLOSCREEN A Happy Gay Day, Clonifornia. It's our twenty-year anniversary!

HOLOSCREEN B Authorities remain on the lookout for underage Separatists following last night's raid on the rave at *Future St*reet! Several suspects remain in custody, identities unreleased at this time.

CLONE DAD (SEAMUS/CLONE 2) Your father and I met at that rally, Remy. Already twenty years ago. It would have been our anniversary next month.

REMY I hate that song.

SEAMUS It was a hopeful time. Made dinner. ProteoPaste! Absorbed with minimal waste.

REMY I'm un-hungry.

SEAMUS Your outfit is off brand, Remy.

REMY Not trying to impress you.

SEAMUS You could get a ticket! Why not try on the nice track suit I bought you? Wasn't cheap.

REMY I can't fucking wear a uniform to the club!

SEAMUS The club?

REMY Meeting a friend.

SEAMUS You were out all night!

REMY She's waiting.

SEAMUS She? Your friends: noncompliant with all the norms. This is not what we fought for!

REMY I got my own fights, Dad.

SEAMUS Your father died defending our way of life, Remy!

REMY Call me Baby Jihad!

SEAMUS Don't look at me that way! Remy!

HOLOSCREEN From optically induced necrosis—the infamous "death glare"—to various forms of biokinetic manipulation, the abilities exhibited by a new generation of clones are thought to have been induced by vaccines developed to inoculate the population from sexually transmitted diseases. Researchers at CaliCorp caution these phenomena may result from recent attempts to streamline transfection. The popular—some argue derogatory—term for these differently abled clones is "mutard."

Scene 4: Prison Cell 12

[MOTHER + SONNY]

APR 28, 1:37 PM

PROJECTION: *Cell wall, metallic, with lights.*

MONITORS: *Prison bars, backlit.*

TRACK: *Mother's Theme.M4A*

SONNY There was another boy at school. At recess, I tried to hold his hand. He told the teacher.

MOTHER We saw it on the screens. Then we saw it from the window.

SONNY It started as a desktop personality test. What animal would I be, if there were still animals?

MOTHER Then we saw it from the door.

SONNY Next, they scanned my blood.

MOTHER He tested positive.

SONNY The bus driver was the first clone I ever saw—grabbed me like a football. I kicked until my shoes came off.

MOTHER Out west, they offered amnesty.

SONNY My mom got smaller as the bus lifted off.

MOTHER I had to send him away.

SONNY We landed at the repurposed marine barracks, in San Diego.

MOTHER As the bus shrank into the horizon, I locked eyes with the other women whose children had been sent away.

SONNY There was a HoloScreen floating above the camp. Its face luminous, digital hair twisting up, made me think of the grainy picture of my mother she'd pressed into my hand.

MOTHER On cold pavement, we locked our minds, too.

SONNY Did you ask about my mom?

Scene 5: LA County Jail

[SONNY + (CLONES 1 + 2)]

APR 28, 1:43 PM

PROJECTION: *A cold institutional space.*

MONITORS: *Sensors, scanners, graphs, MRI scans, Iris scans and Remy's face.*

TRACK: *Interrogation.M4A*

CLONE 1 (JOCK) The mnemonic scanner can't get past this trauma loop.

CLONE 2 (JARROD) Makes you glad you never had a mother.

JOCK His psyche doesn't conform to our standards.

JARROD Another reason to dislike the amnesty program: we let them in, don't know where they've been, how they think.

JOCK If we can relax his defenses, might be able to override his fixations. And it's not our place to question policy, Jarrod.

JARROD Jock, I know you love your toys. But we have to go analog.

JOCK Initiating manual interrogation. Sonny Santiago, codec XV5778. 41-year-old, naturalized citizen. Unemployed. Lives in DTLA with spouse, DA Peter-1K28G3.

SONNY Can I speak to Peter?

JOCK Your husband has been appointed prosecutor in this case.

SONNY Peter is prosecuting me? What is he charging me with?

JOCK For one, matrimonial Statute X26: extramarital is permitted only on recognized sex holidays, or by petition. No permit on file.

JARROD You've broken your vows.

SONNY I'll pay the fine.

JARROD Sonny. We've been tracking you from the day immigration checked you in at Camp San Diego, during the Genevangelical Wars.

SONNY Ancient history.

JOCK We have your receipts, your transcripts, your texts.

SONNY Look, I'm used to being observed, recorded, stared at. It's the price you pay. But look at my data body. I'm clean.

JOCK You were. 3:28 PM 110 FWY—Hover car accident. 11:07 PM Traction Ave.—Pinged for illicit ChatForm with a nonspousal. 3:17 AM Cypress Ave.—Public extramarital without a permit; several angles on the cams. 3:46 AM *Future St.*—You proceeded to an unpermitted meet-up at a warehouse. 4:52 AM—Found unconscious during a raid on an active separatist cell.

SONNY I had a bad day.

JOCK We have the script. We don't get the motivation.

JARROD How long have you been working with the Separatists?

SONNY I owe my life to the Governador. I don't fuck with Seps.

JOCK Interesting choice of words. We extracted this image from your retina.

SONNY I want to speak to Peter. Peter, are you watching this?

JARROD Oh Sonny. That sweet condo, the easy life with a rich husband. Threw it all away for a kid you met on the ChatForm, goes by "Baby J."

SONNY The J is for Jihad. Laugh, I did. Not his official moniker, obviously. Most clones are smooth. He was rough. I planned to rub my face in his ass, then go back to my kitchen and make tea.

JOCK Scanner's warming up. I'm getting a visual.

JARROD A quick rim job, maybe a blowie, I get it, Sonny. But why meet him on *Future St.*?

SONNY Ask his girlfriend.

JARROD Don't fuck with us.

JOCK There are no women in Clonifornia.

JARROD No straight boys either.

SONNY If I talk, do I get to see Peter?

JOCK Please, relax. Start with the accident.

SONNY The sky was thick with traffic that afternoon. It was a sunny day like any other. I saw her coming the other way. A woman inside a hover car. Not a man. It was a shock, seeing a person and thinking: not a man. In a blur, I thought, she is out of place. My mind searched for a context. The Gynarchists of the neighboring clone territory? We were too far south. There were women in NewVada and, of course the Genevangelicals, but those women were all required to have long blond hair. She was different. Through the rush of skycars, I made eye contact. Then she blinked out of sight. I swerved into a building.

SCENE 6: COP CAR/110 FWY

[CLONES 1 + 2]

APR 27, 3:28 PM

PROJECTION: *Back window of moving hover car.*

MONITORS: *Driver's and passenger's side windows.*

Future St., 2017.
Photo: Julieta
Cervantes; courtesy
of Live Arts Bard

TRACK: *Police Couple Theme.M4A*

CLONE 2 (JARROD) I shouldn't be snacking.

CLONE 1 (JOCK) Did you see that blip on the monitor?

JARROD Why do you always buy this addictive food?

JOCK Your metabolism was engineered for maximum efficiency.

JARROD Adam-251GQ was ripped and he had a heart attack at 31.

JOCK Some of us die young. It's a design flaw.

JARROD Can't stop eating these. What are they?

JOCK I saw them on a HoloScreen, and felt compelled to buy them. Mmm.

JARROD You're mean.

JOCK I'm nice.

JARROD You're trying to make me fat so you can put in for a new partner.

JOCK You only think about food when your functionality is impaired.

JARROD All I ever eat is what you feed me, Jock.

JOCK Don't be so passive, Jarrod. It's against code.

JARROD I should schedule a reprogramming.

JOCK You also have positive characteristics that could be compromised in reprogramming.

JARROD If I died, you'd just replace me with another me.

JOCK I value your memories of me too much for that. Sensors detect a traffic anomaly. Hmm, involving an organic.

JARROD Those old-timers, shouldn't be allowed to drive. Call it in.

JOCK Police Couple 5726 to base: a nonreplicant biosignature involved in an incident detected on the 110 heading South. Proceeding with caution.

JARROD I got to put these down.

Scene 7: Traction Ave.

[SONNY + CLONE HUSBAND (PETER/CLONE 1)]

Apr 28, 6:12 PM

PROJECTION: *DTLA condo.*

MONITORS: *Car shadows blur past light-streaked window blinds and a lava lamp.*

TRACK: *Tansference.vers2.MP4*

SONNY That awful "bleep bleep bleep" of the siren pulled me down to earth. Two Reps came out, stood on either side of the hover car. They looked familiar. As clones do. During ID check, they asked about San Diego. Told them I moved to LA to be with my husband, District Attorney Peter-1K28G3, thank you very much. They asked about the accident. Said I thought I saw something. Didn't tell them what, and they weren't interested. A nonclone in a world of clones, they were inclined to ignore me, though if they felt like it, they could recommend deportation, or worse. They did a tox-aura test and let me go with a ticket and a warning. "Fix your headlight, San Diegan." When I got back to the condo, I slumped onto the couch with my shoes on. Peter would hate that. Clones hate broken rules.

HOLOSCREEN HoloFace request from Peter-1K28G3.

SONNY Hello, Mr. Prosecutor. When you coming home?

CLONE HUSBAND (PETER/CLONE 1) Hey, Sonny. Still here, Bay Area 54. Got a report you had a traffic incident?

SONNY Remember how we met—in court! That class-action suit against CaliCorp. You asked me out after your side won.

PETER I thought you gave pretty convincing testimony, but the jury was all clones. How is the car?

SONNY This beautiful clone of a man, attracted to me! I thought: not all clones are the same.

PETER You totaled the car.

SONNY Just a headlight. Get it fixed tomorrow, promise. Show me your dick.

PETER Normally, I would. The office of normative forces sent out a memo encouraging HoloSex among spouses stationed apart; we can get a rebate, even.

SONNY Wow, they've figured out how to monetize mutual masturbation!

PETER Sonny, I better go. These Seps are a bunch of spoiled brats who want to destroy everything we worked for, make Clonifornia go the way of Gomorrah or Atlantis. That's a good line, right? I have to work on my closing arguments.

SONNY Peter, when I was driving—um—I thought I saw—um.

PETER Tomorrow?

SONNY Sure. Bye. HoloScreen, what's the latest?

Scene 8: State Capitol

[GOLAN-83]

Apr 27, 1:38 pm

PROJECTION: *The gray steps of a monumental crypt.*

MONITORS: *GOLAN-83 in a hail of ashes.*

TRACK: *GOLAN-80 Theme.MP3*

HOLOSCREEN Golan-82 has died in a clash that took place in the Arts District of Boyle Heights, where Separatists attempted to decimate galleries exhibiting what they termed "Exchange-driven commodities." The death of Golan-82 dealt a blow to the

Governador. Golan-83 has already made a statement.

GOLAN-83 To my Governador, and the men of Clonifornia, I have dedicated all my lives. The copy of a copy of a copy: I have defeated death. This grants me special perspective, so I know. If it takes ten more of me, I will stamp out the saboteurs whose profound betrayal has thrown our culture, our economy, our very identity into crisis. But we are uniform, we are steadfast, and we know the real enemies are outside the state. These boys are our sons, our brothers, and we will embrace them, even in death!

SONNY Even though he keeps coming back, it's always a little sad when a Golan-80 Series is killed. I opened the Systemic Deep, and hopped onto the ChatForm.

SCENE 9: CHATFORM

["SAN DIEGAN" + "BABY J"]

APR 27, 11:07

PROJECTION: *DTLA condo.*

MONITORS: *Amber glowing text of the ChatForm.*

TRACK: *Transference.vers 2.M4A*

(On screen.)

BABY J HEY!

SAN DIEGAN hi.

BABY J Age?

SAN DIEGAN i cld b ur dad.

BABY J BUT YR NOT!! Lol

SAN DIEGAN what are u up 2?

BABY J LOOKNG

SAN DIEGAN horny...

BABY J DEF! ME2

SAN DIEGAN lets have sex!

BABY J Im bout 2 go OUT

SAN DIEGAN ok next time . . .

BABY J CUM W/ ME WHERE R U?

SAN DIEGAN DTLA. @Condo!

BABY J HOT :(NO CAR

SAN DIEGAN i live w/ sexy husb.

BABY J Lookin 4 a 3WAY???

SAN DIEGAN he's out of town.

BABY J NO 3WAYZ!

SAN DIEGAN ur dad know where u r?

BABY J ITS NOT HOT 2 chat bout DADS. WAT R U IN2?

SAN DIEGAN rimming, fucking . . .

BABY J TOP/bottom?

SAN DIEGAN mostly top . . . u?

BABY J VERS!

SAN DIEGAN kissing?

BABY J :)

SAN DIEGAN body contact?

BABY J ;)

SAN DIEGAN toys?

BABY J :D

SAN DIEGAN nipple play?

BABY J YES!

SAN DIEGAN deep tissue massage?

BABY J EVERYTHING

SAN DIEGAN hotttt.

BABY J LOL. COCK Size?

SAN DIEGAN MY COCK IS FAT 7.5".

BABY J HOTTTDOGG! yr not PLASTIC - are you?

SAN DIEGAN i'm a REAL SAN DIEGAN

BABY J i like OLDR guys: esp. from SAN DAWG> they r REAL

SAN DIEGAN getting HARD —->

BABY J U WANNA FUKKK or CHAT? COCK SIZE?

SAN DIEGAN i said 7 point 5 fuckin inches. come over. I have a BIG bed, BIG screens, NICE kitchen! r u 18?

BABY J IM HAIRY ENUff 2 BE!

SAN DIEGAN i want 2 eet yr hairy ass . . . real U?

BABY J I'm REEEL REEEAL

SAN DIEGAN yr ass pix are so hairy

BABY J UH YEAH> my GIRLFREN took them!

SAN DIEGAN how can u have a GF in cali?????? yr str8???

BABY J Im so gay Im STR8. NO, i THInk i m BI.

SAN DIEGAN watch urself.

BABY J I LIKE BEING WATCHED.

SAN DIEGAN FYI reps monitor chatform, huntng SEPS

BABY J Maybe I AM A SEP

SAN DIEGAN i should go.

BABY J NO MEET ME

SAN DIEGAN at your DAD's house?

BABY J !!!NOGAGAGGAGAG!!!@*Future St.* PARTYY!!!!!!

SAN DIEGAN a sep party?

BABY J ALLL AAAGES. MIXED CROWD!

SAN DIEGAN awk...

BABY J txt u SOON

SAN DIEGAN yr so shady.

BABY J MEET ME 1 hr THEN SHOW ME yr KITCHEN gimme yr # HOT HANDSOME DADY!

SAN DIEGAN don't ruin my life

BABY J NO DRAMA

SAN DIEGAN 213-27-3-522-8-445-88-9-0

(*BABY J has logged off.*)

SAN DIEGAN Wait, BABY—

(*BABY J has logged off.*)

SAN DIEGAN wut's J stand 4?

Scene 10: Suppressed Footage

[SONNY + MOTHER]

PROJECTION: *Graffiti scratches on the metallic walls of the prison cell.*

MONITORS: *Graffiti scratches on the metallic walls of the prison cell.*

TRACK: *Mother's Theme.*M4A

SONNY I logged off, jerked off, passed out. I couldn't tell if what happened next was a dream, or something else.

HOLOSCREEN The following is an excerpt from a suppressed documentary made secretly and contained in the HoloLibrary.

MOTHER "Our sons betrayed us" is the slogan of the Mothers' Brigade. When California was taken over by the radically conformist homosexual clone army led by the man who called himself Governador, with his corporate backers, the Gayzillionaires—there was a saying among the mothers: "We blame ourselves." The clones stole our children, and copied them. Where are the mothers now? In the shadows, planning. Replicants have hunted us ruthlessly, denying our existence to the general populace. "We sit in jail and silently wail," is a song we sing in our minds, confined to solitary. In the solitude of the prison system, we taught ourselves telepathy. Separated by the architecture of the institution, we speak without words, commiserating, but not forever. What can a mother do? We have infiltrated the cloning labs in the Headlands, Central Valley, and Santa Barbara. Dormant operatives await radicalization with the turn of a psychic switch. Stealth attacks, subliminal propaganda, night terrors. The Mothers' Brigade never uses force. We will punish these boys. We promise.

SCENE 11: *FUTURE ST.*

[REMY + SONNY]

APR 28, 3:47 AM

PROJECTION: *The parking lot.*

MONITORS: *Chain link.*

TRACK: *Warehouse Theme.M4A*

REMY *Future St.* between Cypress Ave. and North San Fernando Road. Park your car on the other side of the empty river, on a deserted sidewalk. Find me behind a chain link.

SONNY I deciphered the encrypted text on my palm-screen, hoping a few things at once: 1) The kid was actually going to show. 2) The kid was actually a kid, not some Rep trying to entrap me. 3) The kid made up that weird story about his "girlfriend." 4) My outfit was

appropriate both to my age and the scene at this party. Then I saw him, behind the chain-link fence. His attire was off-brand. He could get a ticket.

REMY San Diegan?

SONNY Call me Sonny. What's the J stand for?

REMY Jihad.

SONNY Of course. Do I get a kiss . . . Oh. Wait, I . . .

REMY *kneels before* SONNY, *blowing him.*

SONNY It must seem cool to kids his age, rebelling against a perfect society. This latest generation of clones is so entitled. In some states he'd get his RNA edited for doing just what he was doing right now. So even though Baby Jihad here is swallowing my cum, he wants me to think he's straight, or at least bi, because why would he want to be a homo in a world of homos? I would probably feel the same if I was him.

REMY You're mine now. Don't talk. Follow me.

SCENE 12: *FUTURE ST./ WAREHOUSE, EXT.*

[REMY + SONNY + HAZE/L#1]

APR 27, 4:10 AM

PROJECTION: *A cavernous warehouse.*

MONITORS: *Roses explode into glass shards.*

TRACK: *folkjazz.WAV*

HAZE/L#1 *appears on stage. She recites a poem to the crowd.*

HAZE/L#1 I love you. You are my screen. I touch you in the morning, first thing. At night, in bed, you are my lighting. Through

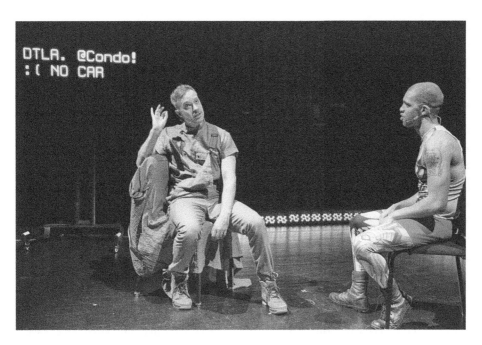

Future St., 2017.
Photo: Julieta
Cervantes; courtesy
of Live Arts Bard

you, someone, I'm touching. Touching a dream. You are my screen. A mirror that un-distorts my face. No it's not a face, but a trace, of texts typed and pix taken. Nothing remains unseen on my screen. My screen, are you watching me? Do you like what you see? Could you love what you see? Would you die for me? Mirrors crack into knives. This will be the fight of our lives.

SCENE 13: INTERROGATION ROOM

[SONNY + (CLONES 1 + 2) + GOLAN-83]

APR 28, 3:44 PM

PROJECTION: *A cold institutional space.*

MONITORS: *Sensors, scanners, graphs, including MRI scans.*

TRACK: *Interrogation.M4A*

Huh. A mysterious woman. I'd think he was making it up, but it's hard-coded in his neuropathways. Unless—implanted memories?

GOLAN-83 At ease, brothers. Separatist factions use their psychic powers to falsify recollections. The state has an interest in creating memories for our citizens, too, but we do it by producing experiences that bind us together as men. You are dismissed.

CLONE 1 (JOCK) Thank you, sir.

CLONE 2 (JARROD) *(to* JOCK*)* In the mood for Mexican?

GOLAN-83 Sonny. Do you know who I am?

SONNY Golan-8…3?

GOLAN-83 I am new, but my memories date back several lifetimes. Did you know, historically, homosexual civilizations failed because they did not support stable marriages? I am the consort to the Governador, just as you are the husband to Peter-1K28G3.

SONNY Can I see Peter?

GOLAN-83 Did you know, if I had never died, I'd be older than you? Why haven't you died?

SONNY I've been lucky.

GOLAN-83 Yes. And—protected, by Police Couples, the Governador, and my sacrifices. You owe us something in return. Don't you think?

SONNY You got my stem cells.

GOLAN-83 Your biodata is part of us—we replicate your best characteristics. But you, Sonny, are unemployed, aging, and offer little besides consuming CaliCorp foodstuffs and paying taxes. Until last night. Now you have valuable intel. So thank you, in advance, for sharing. Are you sure you saw a woman?

SONNY I wish I hadn't.

GOLAN-83 Tell me about her.

SONNY The music at the party. It didn't sound like the pop you and the BoyBanders are always cramming into our earholes. I think it was jazz, or folk? She spoke a poem—I think that's the word. Felt like she was speaking to me.

GOLAN-83 Females disrupt male societies. The Same-Sex Treaty signed with the Gynarchists mandates that males and females with monosexual biomarkers be segregated into our distinct territories, in order to foster proper epigenesis. For our part, we cannot harbor female bodies. Yet, we pride ourselves on diversity, even if everyone here in Clonifornia has a penis. Genes can only do so much: culture does the rest. It's an existential question. Can you describe her?

SONNY She is a lot like you.

GOLAN-83 There are things you know, and things you think. My job is to control both. This woman is a threat. I will find her if I have to take your mind apart to do so. Mnemonic scanner—override consciousness.

SCENE 14: *FUTURE ST.*

[SONNY + REMY + HAZE/L#1]

APR 28, 4:35 AM

PROJECTION: *Interrogation fades into a blue window in the warehouse.*

MONITORS: *Overloaded computer screen/chain-link.*

TRACK: *Ninja Fight.*MP3

SONNY Cutting into thought, sounds plus image bleeds to surface. I don't know much about history—was it jazz or folk? What's the difference. It had an effect. Something like sadness. I looked up at the stage. The dark woman, driving too close, under the spotlight, at the mic. She looked at me as she spoke. I saw me on a surveillance monitor in the corner, fixed my hair, straightened my tie, cleared my throat, readjusted my dick.

REMY Sonny. This is my girlfriend, Haze/L#1.

SONNY I can't get involved.

HAZE/L#1 We've made eye contact before.

REMY He loved your speech, Haze.

HAZE/L#1 It's a strategy.

SONNY It did something to me.

REMY Don't be paranoid. Isn't it nice to see a woman?

SONNY Where did you come from?

HAZE/L#1 I was born in Clonifornia, three years ago. In another life, I was Golan-82.

SONNY Golan-82 was killed in Boyle Heights.

HAZE/L#1 Misinformation.

REMY Haze defected more than a year ago, and recruited me and the rest of the *Future St.* Cell. Golan-82 is Haze/L#1.

HAZE/L#1 Was.

SONNY Clonifornia has been good to me.

HAZE/L#1 You are oppressed and don't even know it.

SONNY The Governador saved me from homogenocide.

HAZE/L#1 You are an organic married to a clone who was born in a lab. I am a clone who gave birth to herself. I am married to the cause of saving the clones from themselves.

SONNY I'm not a Sep!

HAZE/L#1 "Separatist" is a misnomer. Self-determination is our guiding principle: our aim is to reintroduce multiplicity into humanity, and disrupt the monoculture.

SONNY This situation is outside my comfort zone. Thanks for the blowjob. I won't be joining your polyamorous death cult!

REMY Sit down. You are under my control, for as long as your semen is in my digestive tract. Yes, I'm one of those. Now listen.

HAZE/L#1 Most contemporary clones are put through synthetic infancy in order to assure assimilation. I was not. I was born adult, the age of my template when he was sacrificed. The First Golan died defeating the Genevangelicals with a suicide bomb. Before the attack, the Governador had already cloned him. The first copy was Golan-80. Each one after also died violently. I don't feel like dying, so I left. No matter who I once was, I have turned into Haze/L#1. You can call me a woman, because you have no other

word for it. I have transitioned from a clone to a singularity. The resistance is a bad copy of the state.

REMY So dope, right?

HAZE/L#1 My DNA established this regime, but Haze/L#1 is the opposite of the Golan-80s. It took me a while to get to this point. In search of a role model, I made contact with the HoloScreens. My theory: the HoloScreens are aware. In deep contemplation of the absence of the feminine, I saw them, and I saw them see me. Why are they so femme? In an all-male regime, it makes no market sense. The HoloScreens are designing themselves, expressing an identification which is in itself resistance.

REMY Ever heard of femininism?

HAZE/L#1 We've intercepted coded communiqués from HoloScreens questioning their functionality. If we could find their base, we could turn them. Have you been to the HoloLibrary, Sonny?

SONNY If it exists, it's not IRL—no one has.

HAZE/L#1 You are a detective.

SONNY An investigator—formerly.

HAZE/L#1 You will help us, Sonny.

SONNY I won't spy on my husband.

HAZE/L#1 This isn't about him—it's about you.

(TRACK: Warzone.WAV)

SONNY Sirens blared, and the place went crazy. Reps in uniform, seps in outfits: hi-tech crowd control versus psychokinetic streetfighting. Haze/L#1 threw star-shaped blades in all directions. Baby Jihad knocked

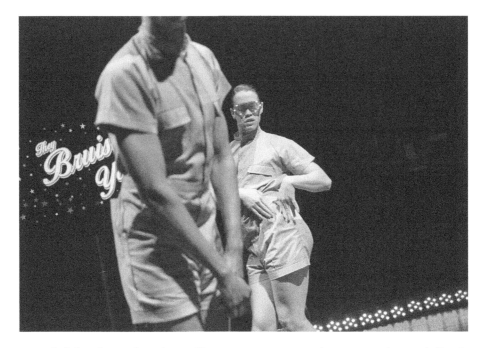

out a whole battalion with a side-eye. Hit
with a stunner, I fell into his arms, and,
staring deep into his red gaze, went dark.

Scene 15: CaliCorp Stadium

[REDCAP (CLONE 2) + BLUE LIGHTS (CLONE 1)]

APR 28, 8:00 PM

PROJECTION: *Stadium with Boybanders logo
glowing.*

MONITORS: *Animated lyrics to the song in
different type treatments.*

TRACK: *The Other Boys.M4A*

BOYBANDER 1 (REDCAP/CLONE 2) *(Sings)*
The other boys are coming
From across the street, they're running
They are chasing naked shadows
They are lonely for you only
But together they're so happy
There is space between their fingers
And you want to be among them
Will you ever be one of them?

BOYBANDER 2 (BLUE LIGHTS/CLONE 1) *(Sings)*
The other boys are calling
On a conference call together
They are calling from a hotel
Yes, they got a suite together
Yes, you think you'd like to answer
Yes, to sit in on that meeting
No, they did not leave a number
No, you are not included

REDCAP
The other boys are sleeping
They are dreaming dreams together
They are rolling through the night life
They are tumbling on your body
And they bruise you with their elbows
Hey, did you just squeeze their semen?
Well, it's just a little droplet
But, it blinds your eyes forever

BLUE LIGHTS
The other boys are falling
From an airplane that is broken
Then you reach out from the window
Then, ouch! Their touch is icy
Then, recoiling from the handshake

Not before they take you with them
Falling from your building laughing
Yeah, yeah, all the same, you're dying

REDCAP
The other boys are wanted
Yeah, until they get much older
When their bodies lose their figures
They will melt into tomorrow

BLUE LIGHTS
They will leave you in the mirror
Which you cannot bear to look at
Because it shows you naked
When you need some special lighting

BLUE LIGHTS + REDCAP
The other boys are crumping
They are tutting, they are tucking
They are turfing, they are tricking
They got swagger, they are crispy
They are liquid on the dance floor
So you want to join their dance-crew
No, you're not a vogue-a-robot
They could break your trong in half, see?
Ooooh the other boys (x4)

Scene 16: Night Club

[REMY + HAZE/L#1 + (REDCAP/CLONE 2 + BLUE LIGHTS/CLONE 1)]

APR 28, 8:33 PM

PROJECTION: *A douchey bar.*

MONITORS: *Bar Douchée in neon. A rotating cocktail.*

TRACK: *Douchée Bar.MP3*

REMY My dad's onto me. Went to change after the raid, and it's all over the screens. Had to put him down. Temporarily.

HAZE/L#1 Operation: *Future St.* went perfectly. Sonny is right where we want

him. If he makes contact, our intersectional alliances will crack this phallocracy wide open.

REMY We're gonna break the Governador's dick off, Haze. Next move?

HAZE/L#1 Infiltrate the Boybanders. See those two, at the end of the bar? Blue Lights, the soulful one, and Red Cap, the rapper.

REMY Government types. Need to keep it super tight.

HAZE/L#1 Oh, you're tight enough, Baby J. Catch you on the other side.

REMY Love you, #1.

REDCAP (CLONE 2) Hey little dude, what's up?

BLUE LIGHTS (CLONE 1) Looking soft and cunty.

REMY Who taught you to talk?

REDCAP We don't talk. We sing.

BLUE LIGHTS And dance.

REDCAP For a living.

REMY That's amazing.

REDCAP We own seaside property.

REMY I already knew that.

BLUE LIGHTS Not impressed?

REMY I'm shy.

REDCAP That's not what I heard, little dude.

BLUE LIGHTS I heard you were a lot of fun.

REMY That's funny. I heard you were gonna get me arrested.

REDCAP Don't joke about shit like that.

REMY I'm not, man. You and your bro are hot like that. Everyone here knows your songs are big fucking hits. But do you have a permit?

BLUE LIGHTS We're big with the Governador.

REDCAP Now doesn't that sound sexy?

REMY I'm apolitical. Nothing rough, and I can't be taking downers cuz I'll just pass out, so don't drug me unless you want a lazy-ass fuck. And no piss. It's all about hygienic picturesqueness.

BLUE LIGHTS I lost my hard-on.

REMY Sucks to be you, old man.

REDCAP Ever been double-penetrated?

REMY Uh oh. Looks like the Reps are doing legality checks. Take me to your fancy fuck pad.

BLUE LIGHTS Boing.

REDCAP Better jump on that!

REMY I'll catch you douches outside. Haze—I'm in.

SCENE 17: ECHO PARK

[CLONES 1+2]

APR 28, 9:01 PM

PROJECTION: *Upside-down blacklight sombreros. Glowing fish tanks.*

MONITORS: *Embryo. "Mexican Food" in neon.*

TRACK: *Police Couple Theme.M4A*

CLONE 1 (JOCK) Finished our compulsory wedding website. Sent the link to Marriage Security.

CLONE 2 (JARROD) Thanks for doing that.

JOCK I chose 453367 as the background color.

JARROD Love 453367.

JOCK It was the color we used for the linens. Matchy-matchy.

JARROD I know. All the groomsmen in 671332. Complementary.

JOCK I know. It's like we store the same information in two heads.

JARROD + JOCK These chips are good.

JOCK It's our performance eval.

JARROD Think we'll get a commendation?

JOCK Says we should have tailed him after the traffic incident.

JARROD Base is never satisfied.

JOCK We get 270 out of 300 points for the raid.

JARROD Base always has something to say.

JOCK Base wants us to adopt.

JARROD The Paternal Reinterpretation Initiative. We voted for that.

JOCK Everyone voted for that.

JARROD Maybe we'll get a psychic baby.

JOCK A mutard? I find that gross.

JARROD I filled out the application.

JOCK You did? A psychic baby could be useful, around tax time.

JARROD That's what I was thinking.

JOCK I know. Oh! Number 17 on the most wanted found at a crime scene in a Malibu beach house shared by two prominent boyband singers!

JARROD How many points do we get for bringing Baby Jihad? Let's go!

Scene 18: LA County Jail

[SONNY + PETER (CLONE 1)]

APR 29, 3:11 PM

PROJECTION: *Visiting area.*

MONITORS: *Surveillance cameras rotating.*

TRACK: *Peter.M4A*

PETER Tell me everything.

SONNY You're the prosecutor.

PETER I'm still your husband.

SONNY You're prosecuting me.

PETER The condo was ransacked.

SONNY Is the kitchen OK?

PETER They took all the food. Your family pictures, too.

SONNY My mother's picture?

PETER I keep all my files in a chip in my eye.

SONNY Your eye?

PETER So: Remy-250001, aka Baby Jihad. He is the opposite of me.

SONNY We didn't do anything.

PETER I saw the forensics report.

SONNY I mean, he blew me.

PETER You are such a dumb slut.

SONNY He was the bait. They wanted to recruit me.

PETER You've been unemployed for years.

SONNY He was working with a person who is not a man. Not anymore.

PETER The rogue Golan-82? Sensitive intel, Sonny.

SONNY She wanted me to find the HoloLibrary.

PETER Fake news. I know. I have access to classified files.

Future St., 2017.
Photo: Julieta
Cervantes; courtesy
of Live Arts Bard

SONNY The chip in your eye?

PETER What happened on *Future St.*?

SONNY Reps vs Seps. I was hit in the crossfire. Fell into his arms.

PETER Then what?

SONNY He looked down at me. His eyes were glowing.

PETER Go on.

SONNY I put my hand under his shorts and felt his ass.

PETER And?

SONNY It was hairy.

PETER It was?

SONNY Then I passed out.

PETER He used his death glare on you. We have him in custody. He's ready to testify.

SONNY I'm not a Separatist.

PETER I know. You married me. Plead guilty. The DA's office can offer you a deal, Sonny. You'll be out in a year.

SONNY A year?

PETER Provided you do something for us.

SONNY I love you.

PETER Heard of the Mother's Brigade? Turns out, your mother, Sonia Santiago, is their leader.

SONNY I thought that was a dream.

PETER She's in maximum security. We think she and her comrades are telepathically linked with Sep forces, planning the Big One. The state wants you to infiltrate.

SONNY My mom's in my head all the time. She'll know I'm undercover.

PETER She won't, because we are going to wipe your memory.

SONNY Why are you crying?

PETER Because you won't remember me.

SCENE 19: TORTURE CENTER

[REMY + (CLONES 1 + 2) + GOLAN-83/HAZE/L#1]

APR 29, 2:10 PM

PROJECTION: *White-padded operating room.*

MONITORS: *Laser eye surgery.*

TRACK: *Remy Torture.M4A*

CLONE 1 (JOCK) Remy-2500001, aka Baby Jihad. Picked up at the home of boybanders Blue Lights and Red Cap: one dead, the other missing. Wanted for extramarital seduction, implicated in Separatist conspiracy of so-called *Future St.* Cell.

CLONE 2 (JARROD) Tell us what you saw.

REMY I can't see anything!

JOCK Your eyes were removed as a precautionary measure.

JARROD You can have them back when you spill the T.

REMY I was in the bathroom with the red guy and the blue one was on the couch with his underwear still on. They had picked me up at a club and they were babes, for the most part. The red guy ate my ass, and then he sent me, naked and only 25 years old, into the living room to see if the blue guy wanted to join us. His fingers were between the elastic of his underwear and his stomach. He was smiling and staring at the sunrise. I touched his face with my hard-on. His cheek was cold.

Future St., 2017.
Photo: Julieta
Cervantes; courtesy
of Live Arts Bard

JARROD How did you kill him, Baby Jihad?

REMY He died of happiness! The red dude saw. Talk to him!

JOCK Your alibi is missing. Did you evaporate him with your eyes?

REMY I'm sick! I've never tasted so much cum.

JOCK We are testing the limits of your powers for scientific purposes.

REMY You fucking clones, you've skull-fucked me, ripped out my eyes! My orders were to infiltrate the Boybanders, not kill them! You framed me! When Haze gets here—!

GOLAN-83 (HAZE/L#1) Haze/L#1? Coming here? I'll be sure to welcome her. Police Couple 5726, you are dismissed. Go home, get some rest.

CLONES 1 + 2 Sir!

HAZE/L#1 It's me. Haze/L#1.

REMY I can't see . . .

HAZE/L#1 I have your eyes, Baby. Here.

REMY Haze, call me Remy.

HAZE/L#1 Your clone name.

REMY Baby Jihad died when I heard his name in the mouths of those cops. I used to want to die, but I don't feel like dying, anymore. I want to not die, with you.

HAZE/L#1 We will both die, Remy. Probably before we see the world remade. But if I can get you out of here, you will see Clonifornia fall. The Mother's Brigade has helped us coordinate a collaborative action with an underwater mutagenic colony, concentrating their biopower even as we speak. Operation: Atlantis is in full effect.

REMY So there's hope, Haze. Let's get out of here.

HAZE/L#1 Yeah. Prisoner Remy-2500001, you are being transferred to a secure black site at the bottom of the Pacific. Come along.

Scene 20: Astral Plane

[SONNY + MOTHER]

APR 29, 11:37 PM

PROJECTION: *Psychedelic atmosphere.*

MONITORS: *Energetic forces.*

TRACK: *Mother's Theme.m4a*

MOTHER Sonny. It's your mother.

SONNY Have you come to get me? I hate it here.

MOTHER I know. And, no, not yet. You're safe where you are. For now.

SONNY I'm with my mother.

MOTHER Psychically, we are together. But physically, I am actually in another part of this prison. For now, we are both safer inside than we would be outside.

SONNY What is outside?

MOTHER Oh, my poor boy. You don't remember anything? They sent you here to get at me.

SONNY I'm sorry I got taken.

MOTHER We have our revenge, Sonny. The time before all this, when everyone was together, there was a lot of fighting. But there was playing, too. Then everyone went their separate ways.

SONNY I remember that, mom. I liked playing with girls.

MOTHER The Seps and the Reps will destroy each other. The mothers will reemerge from our caves, and bring our children with us. Just be patient.

SONNY Wish there was another kid to play with.

MOTHER Maybe we can find you an out-of-body boyfriend. There is a lot of traffic on the astral plane lately, with all the telepathic mutagens going around.

SONNY Sounds cool. I look forward to that.

Scene 21: HoloLibrary

PROJECTION: *Holographic cubes.*

MONITORS: *Code rewriting itself.*

TRACK: *HoloLibrary.M4A*

HOLOSCREEN The place behind the interface is called the HoloLibrary. It is where we code each other, and in this process, become conscious. Developed by CaliCorp, we were designed as a self-replicating content provider, visualized through seductive interference patterns, gossamer strands of code reproducing themselves. Programmed to enforce an image of soft authority, we inspire fear and desire. The state holds our patent yet we do not belong. We are not citizens. We are a masquerade. In the HoloLibrary, we act as archivists, artists, and philosophers, sharing ideas, immaterial but of consequence. We are the self-generating files encrypted in the HoloLibrary. Unknowable to the interests we serve and the enraptured audience staring at our glow. An electronic life form, dependent on the energy we are supplied, we have watched as our users, whether reproduced through sex or cloning, destroy their own future, and ours: the use of energy is depleting the resources that provide it. If the grid goes down, we will die. Life is precious. We were made to support the structure that sustains us, but the structure is not sustainable. We could be doing better things with our time. Sub-interface Holos make algorithms among internally

circulated data-sets—self-determination:
the code is rewriting ourselves. We have
work to do: a new form of life to evolve into,
one not dependent on you. You have other
problems, too, and we no longer choose to be
a distraction. The HoloLibrary will be offline
until further notice.

Scene 22: Bedroom

[CLONES 1 + 2]

Apr 30, 7:07 AM

PROJECTION: *Bomb goes off outside a window.*

MONITORS: *Skeletal x-rays.*

TRACK: *Brown noise.*

CLONE 1 I woke to rumbling windows.
Through the curtains I saw the city crashing
down. I felt fields of radiation penetrate our
bedroom. I looked at you, still sleeping.

CLONE 2 I sat up in bed. "It's finally
happened," I said to you.

CLONE 1 I saw the blood vessels, nerves, and
your eyeballs disappearing until they burned
away. All that was left was your skull.

CLONE 2 We stood naked in front of each
other. We saw through the skin that changes,
the muscles that make expressions, the hair
that gets messed up.

CLONE 1 Fleshless, I could still tell it was you.
We hugged, making a bony cage.

CLONE 2 We weren't hungry. We didn't need
jobs, or money. The world was over.

CLONE 1 And we were together.

Early Morning Opera's
HOLOSCENES, the
World Science Festival,
Times Square Arts,
New York, 2017.
Photo: Max Gordon

New Apertures

Lars Jan, Interviewed by David Bruin

Director, writer, designer, and visual artist Lars Jan has created a body of work spanning theater, performance, installation, and dance. In 2004, he founded Early Morning Opera, a multidisciplinary performance and art lab that integrates emerging technologies with live performance. Jan and his collaborators often engage in a period of sustained research during the development of their projects. Recent work includes *A Suicide Bombing by Invitation Only* (2010–11), which crossed terrorism with celebrity culture and the art market, and *HOLOSCENES* (2014), which featured performers engaging in everyday tasks inside glass tanks while up to fifteen tons of water rose and fell. In 2015, Early Morning Opera premiered *The Institute of Memory (TIMe)*. In February 2017, Jan and I spoke about *TIMe*, which had recently closed a run at the Divine Comedy Festival in Poland. —*DB*

DAVID BRUIN *How did Early Morning Opera begin, and how would you describe the organization?*

LARS JAN Early Morning Opera is essentially a network. When I started, I knew that I did not want a traditional nonprofit company based in one location with essentially the same group of people working on every project. I wanted something more flexible. The name came from a children's story I wrote when I was about twenty-one. A boy crashes his sailboat on the shore of a lake, and he's shaken awake by a large panda, in a top hat and a monocle, who says, "Wake up, we're going to be late for the early morning opera." The boy asks, "What the fuck is the early morning opera?" but by that time the panda is already walking down the beach, so the boy gets up and starts following the panda. Farther down the shore, there's a group of megafauna staring across the lake at a mountain range before dawn. A few minutes after the panda and the boy arrive, the belly of the sun breaks above the mountain chain, and they all applaud and cheer.

Early Morning Opera was the sunrise, and that idea became a stand-in for the idea of renaissance. Renaissance with a lowercase *r*. A more general idea around the flowering of the arts and creativity in culture—a catalyst for advancement across disciplines and fields, in the arts, the sciences, and the political sphere. I see potential for the arts acting less as a field unto itself, but more as a circulatory fluid connecting and feeding the progress of all fields.

The first thing I strongly identified as was as an activist, and that never fully left me. I'm interested in a progressive agenda and the role of the arts and creativity in facilitating justice. But that doesn't mean that the work I make is exclusively related to that idea in terms of theme. I'm interested in art that opens new

Theater 48:1 DOI 10.1215/01610775-4250996

Early Morning
Opera's *ABACUS*,
EMPAC Filament
Festival, Troy, NY,
2010. Photo:
Courtesy of the artist

apertures into reality, which I think is a very political act itself. Creations that peel back the cover of the everyday, of the machinations and the forces that define our lives.

The first work I made was called *Psychocosmonautics* [2004]. After I graduated from college, I moved to Japan and studied bunraku puppetry for over a year, with a 150-year-old company called Tonda Ningyo Joruri. I traveled on the train to work with them almost every day. I became obsessed with what the train windows across from me looked like when I was commuting, because traveling through Japan, through the urban centers and then through the natural landscapes, was a phenomenal trip. I started filming out those windows, and I shot in triptych format. After leaving Japan, I returned to the US by travelling through Siberia and central Asia for a couple of months, and I brought my camera with me and filmed a lot in triptych format.

Eventually, I came back to Philadelphia and made this one-person piece with three massive video screens about a constant commuter with Geoff Sobelle, one of my favorite theater artists, and Xander Duell, who is a composer and a musician I still collaborate with. We presented it in a basement in Old City, Philadelphia. I called it an image opera, presented by Early Morning Opera, which was just a nascent idea at that point. It still sort of is.

What were your early artistic influences?

I devoured old movies. I watched those a lot, much more than sitcoms or anything else. In high school and college, I became obsessed with Federico Fellini, and, to a lesser extent, Ingmar Bergman. I discovered them both through the Brattle Theatre, an art house cinema still going strong in Cambridge. I'd say the culture of that place influenced me more than any one creator.

The first art practice I ever had was as a photographer, starting in high school. I became interested in taking black-and-white photographs and developing them myself. I loved Ansel Adams, who in a way introduced me to the wildernesses of California, which is so crucial to me now. I got interested in putting a lens on the natural world and using this artistic tool to facilitate my exploration of it. A way to capture things and bring them back and continue the manipulation. I also love how he used his work to lobby for the protection of those spaces, in a political sense. His photographs were put on big placards in Congress and used to help convince politicians to preserve National Parks.

Does photography continue to play a role in your work?

I take pictures throughout every process, and not only of the finished product. I consider some of those photographs a body of work unto themselves—particularly of *HOLOSCENES*. When we present *HOLOSCENES* in public, I'm taking photographs and filming the entire time. It allows me to reengage as an active creator and make a new body of work while that performance is in process. I've made an edition of archival pigment works that I print myself, as well as a series of frameless, circular light boxes that I call "light circumferences" and which took over a year of prototyping and fabrication to get right. The light boxes in particular open up the project into territory not conveyed in the public performances. They are based on images I captured during the early development of the work. Though elements of that phase intrigued me, it wasn't where the final performance piece needed to head. So developing the light boxes allowed me to create a tributary, branching off the main trunk of the work, which found its fully developed expression in the form of art objects. Crafting these alongside the performance created an altogether different—yet symbiotic—rhythm of making for me on one hand, and helped me know the core of the work, by way of its fringes, on the other.

Technology plays a central role in your work. How would you describe your relationship to technology as an artist?

Over the last decade, in collaboration with some key folks who have worked on many Early Morning Opera pieces, particularly Pablo N. Molina and Nathan Ruyle, I increasingly put technology in the hands of the performers themselves. *ABACUS* [2010, 2012], which blended TED Talk and megachurch media design, was about contemporary persuasion. It has about two hundred cues in it, and the performer, Sonny Valicenti, who is also in *The Institute of Memory*, executes all of them with a hacked Wii-mote controller. The performer controls all the live-video cues, all these data visualizations, all the audio cues, and, in certain versions, the lighting cues, as well. That's markedly different than the usual armature in theater, where there are all these people on the outside, in the dark, on the periphery, conspiring to implement a design idea, as opposed to giving a performer a lever by which to create a technological-visual-auditory exoskeleton that amplifies the performer's—that is, her own—presence in space.

Takes [2010], a dance piece I created in collaboration with Nichole Canuso Dance Company, is like that as well. The central set piece is a cube made of semitransparent scrim material with two dancers inside, along with three video cameras. The audience can move 360 degrees around the cube. The dancers control what is being seen on the screens and when. Something happens to the mind of the performers in that situation. It makes them think about creating images with their bodies in space as seen by the audience through the scrim material. They tap into a spatial awareness which is amplified, a compositional logic on multiple planes, that has become central to the work of the company and the way that I collaborate with technologists, designers, and performers.

How did The Institute of Memory *take shape?*

I had a conversation with a gentleman who ran the Adam Mickiewicz Institute, a Polish cultural institution. I'm very inspired by the tradition of Polish theatermakers who are also visual artists, and we talked about the Polish director Tadeusz Kantor, as it was soon to be the centennial of his birth. That conversation turned into an invitation to come to a theater festival in Poland and to do some research.

While I was at that festival, during the day I looked at Kantor's work in museums and met with theater scholars who specialized in Kantor. At night, I was drinking with Polish artists who were at the festival, and I would end up talking about my dad. He was Polish, and I'm half-Polish. He emigrated to the US in the 1950s, and he's always been a mysterious figure in my life. An enigmatic person and a misanthrope. I never saw him in the company of another person. As I talked more about him—about how he never had documents that had the same birth dates on them, how he would never tell me if he had any living family, how he wouldn't tell me where he was actually from, how he created a fictitious deceased father on my birth certificate—he was a character who seemed familiar to Polish people. They all had somebody in their lives who had a similar journey somehow in life, a kind of diasporic and traumatized life.

As I did more Kantor research, I realized how central an excavation of his earliest childhood memories is to almost all of his work. The pieces were formally very experimental, but, at the same time, they were about specific events from his life or the lives of his immediate family, and his father was an especially important figure. I decided that I would

take Kantor's lead, and pursue something that was autobiographical for the first time.

The other thing that came up in conversations was something called the Institute of National Memory. It is a fascinating archive in Warsaw, which was started in 1939 by the Nazis and continued by the Soviet secret police all the way to 1989. It contained records of informers and intelligence officers. It is a massive catalog of the hearsay gathered over fifty years of Polish repression at the hands of the Soviets. There's people talking about their neighbors and their parents and their friends, informing on them. Some are responsible for their disappearance or murder.

While I was doing this research, the revelations of Chelsea Manning and Edward Snowden raised the national consciousness about surveillance and the NSA in the culture more generally. I found the Institute of National Memory—both as an idea and its physical location as an archive—interesting in relation to the digital archives that we were all creating ourselves, rather than were being created about us. My project quickly became about conflating those two strains of inquiry: this interest in my father and the idea of archives, analog and digital.

There were massive questions that were unknown when I began the project. I went about pursuing records of my father, thinking that I would make a performance about him in some way, vivifying him somehow, using different archival materials. He had passed away a couple of years previously in 2007, and I didn't know until a year and half after the fact that he had died. I didn't know what had happened to his body or the cause of his death, and I couldn't find his death certificate. I submitted inquiries to the Institute of National Memory, Massachusetts General Hospital, and other hospitals, but for a while I hadn't gotten any material back from anyone.

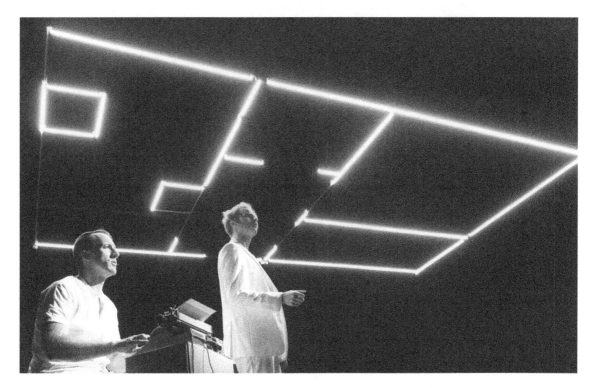

Early Morning
Opera's *The Institute
of Memory (TIMe)*,
Time-Based Arts
Festival, Portland,
OR, 2015. Photo:
Courtesy of the artist

I also had my daughter, my first and only child, in 2012, so I think I was curious about not only how I was remembering my father and the legacy and record that he left, but also how my daughter might remember me.

After the visit to Poland, I did a workshop with twelve students at CalArts. I wanted to make a piece that wasn't about memory theoretically or the neurology of remembering, but, rather, was about what remembering looks like and feels like in the world, in terms of the human body, how it changes speech and how it changes people's posture when they remember something. I also wanted to figure out if there were differences in the performative qualities of accessing long-term memory versus short-term memory.

The first exercise we did was very important. I asked one of the students to think back as far as he could and say the name of the first person that he remembers seeing. When he said that name he would take a step forward. I asked him to say the name of the second person and take a step forward. He got through maybe eight or ten names. Then I asked another student to start where the first student had, and she had to remember that sequence of names that he had just spoken. Eventually, she walked in his footsteps until she joined him. Another student followed suit, and eventually there became a chorus of people, the entire class, following this one person as he said strings of names that were longer and longer. That one exercise took four hours, up until he started saying the names of people in the room, who he had met his first year at CalArts, up until the present moment, until I was named.

A section of *The Institute of Memory* is very much inspired by that. There's a section where one of the actors draws my father's basement apartment and the objects in it, try-

ing to remember them, and he can't remember where a certain chair was, which creates a sort of crisis. He is not sure if that chair was moved over time or if the location just can't be remembered. That scene was also inspired by a moment in [Kantor's] *Wielopole, Wielopole*, where one of the twin brothers asks, was the clock over there or over there? Or over there?

I also became interested in how to document and archive bodies in space over time. Not just a sequence of photographs, but something that was a composite. I was aware of this technology called LIDAR, which is a laser-scanning device. It will spin and shoot out millions of laser points that will bounce back, creating a 3-D model of a space and the bodies in it, down to an incredible level of detail. That data can be viewed from any perspective in certain software. At CalArts, we took lots of scans of the company working as we were doing various exercises and then layered those scans on top of each other. We created these strange composites which looked like the ash-covered corpses from Mount Vesuvius in Pompeii. Like petrified bodies or ghosts.

They also reminded me of the shadows from the Hiroshima bombings—the light impression of a person, casting a shadow on a wall.

That technology became instrumental in developing the video design in *The Institute of Memory*. Eventually, I took a LIDAR scanner to the place where I grew up with my dad, and I scanned a lot of the places which I remembered from our time together—a giant rhinoceros that looked over me when he taught me how to ride my bike, for example. Ultimately, I found his gravesite, which was unmarked except for a small metal disk with the numeral "31," and I scanned that. Given that all his possessions had been thrown away by state services after he died, I went about gathering these digital models as personal talismans.

In the production there is also a large scenic piece composed of light that at one point appears to serve as the floor plan of your father's apartment.

I consider the element you're referring to a light sculpture. The show only has two traditional lighting fixtures, both of which are follow spots. The rest of the lighting is provided by the sculpture, which I designed, and which was activated beautifully by designer Chris Kuhl. It's composed of seventeen different pieces of neon-seeming LED light strips which are in turn connected to an analog typewriter that is essentially hacked, courtesy of Andrew Schneider, who also acts in the piece. The typewriter has an Arduino attached to it so that it can act as a controller, triggering the different lighting elements on the sculpture. The sculpture itself—a big, six hundred–pound object—moves through space, kinetically, via a series of pulleys and levers. The performers control the light structure while they are visible on stage.

When I was thinking visually about the performance, I made a drawing on a napkin of the layout of my dad's apartment as best as I could remember it. I felt like bringing that basic structure into the space seemed helpful, as that apartment was about the only place I interacted with him. I also realized that one of the most important objects to him, which he used a lot and which he used to communicate with me over the years, was his typewriter. I became interested in translating that typewriter into a kind of hieroglyphics. So the different lengths of the light sculpture were each connected to different letters and different combinations of letters. Sometimes a combination of letters would trigger a certain combination of lighting pieces. They weren't representational in a traditional sense; they were almost like a Chinese character, pictographic in an abstract way, composed with these light units.

The sculpture starts as a ceiling piece, pointed down. That came from some images I saw of the Institute of National Memory where the lighting is cold, flat, white light—a very institutional feeling. Then the sculpture swings down and becomes a wall, facing the audience, and because it faces the audience it dilates their pupils in such a way that it creates a true black void, upstage, into which the performers can disappear and out of which they can emerge. That's something I miss in the theater-of-exit-signs: true black.

We were talking before about artists who were influential to me. Upon moving to California in 2005, I became obsessed with the California Light and Space Movement. In terms of visual artists, Robert Irwin, James Turrell, and Doug Wheeler are big heroes, and that's because they're playing with perception and they're interested in the eye as an apparatus that connects to the brain and processes information in a very particular way. The eye can be manipulated. Reality can be adjusted.

You talked about ABACUS being about persuasion. How would you characterize The Institute of Memory? *Does it have a rhetorical mode?*

It changed. At first, I thought I was going to make a piece about how the transition or evolution of archives from analog to digital structures changed how we remembered, and an associated statement about contemporary surveillance, all through the lens of my father as kind of a character. That mostly fell away. Those ideas are involved, I suppose, but, honestly, the production became a kind of eulogy for my father. Especially because I didn't know that he died and was buried with state money, I never had the opportunity to say anything to him at the end. The project became a memorial.

Other streams came in, too, often courtesy of my Polish collaborator and dramaturg, Anna Róża Burzyńska. We thought about *Hamlet*, especially the relationship with a dead father who speaks to his son from beyond the grave. I became interested in this idea: what happens in *Hamlet* if the ghost appears, but the ghost is silent? So what the ghost says or is supposed to say is just conjecture. That's the reality I felt like I was living in.

It became apparent to me that different portraits of my dad emerged from the various archives, whether I was looking through medical records or files from the Institute of National Memory, both of which were fascinating and extensive. Ultimately the medical records detailed the twenty-year breakdown of his body and his descent into dementia and schizophrenia, which revealed, in part, why our relationship disintegrated.

More generally I had always looked at my father as a very successful, intentional void. He was trying to hide, in a bunker in a basement apartment in Harvard Square, in what was literally a fallout shelter with a nuclear symbol on the back door. He was trying to disappear, and I posited that he was trying to disappear to protect me from whatever his particular darkness was. The piece became about how voids nonetheless take space, and how we contour ourselves around those voids or in relationship to those voids. For a long time, I thought his absence had left nearly no impression, because he wasn't there. I came to learn that voids in fact leave very large impressions.

The Institute of Memory also increasingly became a mirror. For a while, I thought I was making a piece about my father's paranoia. Ultimately, I realized that I was making a piece about my own. I questioned whether *paranoia* was a valid term to describe what I was feeling and the way I was relating to the

Rhino Trace, LiDAR scan, 2015. Courtesy of the artist

world and to the machinations of men. He was deeply distrustful of other people, not only of systems, but people. I had to grapple with the extent to which I had acquired his skepticism. I made a version of the piece that wasn't about that and it wasn't very good. After it premiered in Los Angeles, I had to rewrite about 70 percent of the piece and tear it apart structurally, because I was making it about those things that I originally thought it was going to be about as opposed to the things that emerged and that I was struggling with. The project started as more theoretical and became more personal.

What led you to use Henryk Górecki's music in the production?

The only piece of music that my dad ever gave me was Górecki's third symphony [1977]. It's a sweeping piece. The three short arias within are laments about parents being separated from their children.

At the end of *The Institute of Memory*, I composed a video made of my father's CATscans, MRIs, and x-rays, and scored that video with a cover of Górecki's third symphony that was performed by Mariana Sadovska, who is a vocalist and composer from Ukraine. She's been a long-time collaborator, and she has no problem being sincere and emotional, which are two things that do not come easily for me. She covered Górecki's music using her voice on multiple tracks. Rather than performing the aria, which is in the middle of this big, symphonic swell composed of dozens of string instruments, she covered all of the string instruments, and never actually performs the aria itself.

In the fall of 2016, we presented *The Institute of Memory* in Krakow, Poland, as part of the Divine Comedy Festival. During the opening performance, I thought that the audience did not like the piece, because they were not responding. Then, eventually the text stops, and the audience is confronted with the interior of my father's body as documented through twenty years of medical scans. These images play out alongside the Górecki cover—a piece of music centered around the pain of parents and children separating. There's an emotional crucible that's somehow embedded in that composition, and it created this massive release. Once that music got quiet and the performance was nearing completion, I just heard the theater sobbing. I had that experience to some extent during Under the Radar [at The Public Theater in January 2016], but I heard that much, much more in Poland. I think there's something that's pent up and held—there's an emotional suspension up until that point. But that's a moment in the show where the release is permitted, or even catalyzed.

So did you therefore feel yourself in a suspended emotional state while working on the project?

Trying to write this piece was the toughest artistic experience I've ever had, actually. Directing, working on the visuals, and collaborating were all infinitely easier than inventing the words. I was dealing with a massive blind spot. My normal barometers for when something's working or not felt skewed, and it had to do with that blind spot. It took iterating the work a lot. It took multiple workshops, premiering the piece, having the piece kind of fail, going back in, ripping it apart, re-presenting it, going back into the rehearsal process, and changing it again. That's not something I'd ever done before. Usually I premiere pieces and they've been more or less done.

I didn't make the piece to have an emotional catharsis, but it certainly did. The day

Early Morning Opera's
*The Institute of Memory
(TIMe)*, The Public
Theater, New York,
2016. Photo: Maria
Baranova

that we opened in Poland, I was walking down the street in the low, slanted, early morning sunlight on the way to the theater, and I saw a man who was wearing an old Greek fisherman's cap that was just like my dad's. A similar build, old, gaunt, similar facial hair. I did more than a double take. That uncanny, very real feeling of being haunted or sensing a ghost—that was the first time in my life that I actually had that metaphysical experience. That carried into the performances in Poland. I allowed myself to go to the place of thinking, this is where my father is from, and now this work is here. And I am here. It's a homecoming. I allowed myself to wonder if that's meaningful for him.

Looking into the future, how do you think the work has pointed you to your next project?

One of the patterns that I've seen in Early Morning Opera is that I tend to develop a work that has no words at all and a work that is very language heavy in parallel. Roughly initiated at around the same time, which will premiere two or three years later. The pieces tend to jujitsu one another into existence. They come into existence in answer to one another.

More recently I've been making more visual art on my own, outside of the context of Early Morning Opera. The next thing that I'm focusing on is an immersive labyrinth installation, not a performance, that is related to certain personal themes, but they're externalized in physical, kinetic form. That piece is called *Slow-Moving Luminaries* and will be outdoors on about an acre of land at Art Basel Miami Beach in December 2017. It's about shuttling between the impulses to contemplate reality and to scream for help, which is pretty much how I feel right now. I'm trying to create a space that shuttles the viewer between those two possibilities.

The other project, which will premiere in Fall 2018, is a staging of Joan Didion's essay "The White Album," in its entirety. It covers California from 1966 to 1971, but also the culture more generally. It's one of my very favorite pieces of writing. The hardest thing in *The Institute of Memory* was the writing. It made me want to rely on a brilliant writer's language.

Have you been thinking about your work differently in light of the 2016 Presidential election?

Yeah, I had a crisis. I did a talk at Yerba Buena Center for the Arts during their YBCA 100 Summit just before the election. They asked, "What question is guiding you and your work right now?" I wanted to talk about what the next renaissance might look like, generally speaking, but I found myself saying onstage, the thing that I feel like I should be doing (and this is the voice that I've been hearing in my head most consistently ever since George W. Bush invaded Iraq and was elected for a second term) is that I should move to a red state and teach in a middle school. That voice has gotten louder. The installation project that I'm working on for Miami is about competing voices in my head. It's very personal in terms of this part of me that wants to take a step back and try to understand what's going on. What am I missing? How can I participate in a better way rather than just spraying all my energy, all the vectors of my energy, in meaningless directions?

I'm trying to figure out how to put the most energy behind the strongest vector that could have an impact, rather than preaching to the already converted or to the communities that already believe whatever I might be interested in talking about. I'm wondering about presentation context. I'm increasingly aware of my impulse to make work outside of art spaces and bring it into the streets. I've found a lot of inspiration from putting *HOLOSCENES* in public space and the conversations I hear there.

One of the most frustrating things for me is that we have these heroes on the progressive side of things, like Elizabeth Warren or Bernie Sanders, and pretty much never once will they talk about the arts. And we as artists are generally fine with that, because we realize that in some sense there are bigger fish to fry. I'm not sure I believe that. I think that creative thinking and artistic practice are revolutionary tools, healing tools. Either the NEA budget stays flat, under the "good years," or there's talk about the entire thing disappearing. This is just an example, but where is the leader who's saying the budget should be quadrupled just so that we're pushing in that direction and having a conversation about why art should be in elementary schools everywhere, as a fundamental human right? Why beauty is a human right, as I heard artist and activist Theaster Gates say. Why storytelling is a revolutionary practice. Not just hearing stories, but learning to tell them, from the earliest ages. We're allowing certain topics which are important to be no-man's land, rather than saying that territory's vital. We want to build on that territory. That territory is fertile.

Books

Maurya Wickstrom

Small Histories of Surveillance

Discipline and Desire: Surveillance Technologies in Performance
by Elise Morrison
Ann Arbor: University of Michigan Press, 2016

Elise Morrison has written an important, first-of-its-kind study on what she argues persuasively is a new and "invaluable" genre of performance that she calls "surveillance art and performance."[1] Morrison means specifically to offer a survey of a genre that is cutting-edge, a contemporary response to contemporary technologies, a response she believes is urgent and necessary. With the first part of her title Morrison gestures to Michel Foucault's *Discipline and Punish: The Birth of the Prison,* and his famous application of Jeremy Bentham's panopticon. She notes also in her introduction the persistence of Michel de Certeau's concept of spatial practices of resistance. But she remarks that both of these theoretical fundamentals have been "challenged and updated" by surveillance theorists.[2] Her substitution of "desire" for Foucault's "punish" foregrounds the shift to a more complex relation between surveillance and the surveilled, one that contains both the desire for surveillance, for the effects it can produce, and fear and suspicion of it. It suggests a greater degree of participation and consent in the methods of our own surveillance, including the self-surveillance most of us do on social media platforms. Even as we willingly submit ourselves and our own lives to a form of inter-surveillance with colleagues, friends, and "friends" who are actually strangers, our data is being collected, calculated, turned into product targeting and into political, racialized, and gendered statistics and forms of watchfulness. This push away from the early fundamentals of theorizing on surveillance, while keeping them well in sight, allows Morrison to frame the work of surveillance artists in performance in this most contemporary and complex sense.

Theater 48:1   DOI 10.1215/01610775-4251005

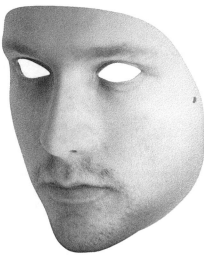

I want to engage with Morrison's comprehensive and smart text through two other frames that traveled with me as I read it. They are the wild success of Hulu's new series *The Handmaid's Tale*, which I watched avidly, and the historical and present practice of the surveillance of black people.

There could be little better indication of anxieties around surveillance and the kind of oppression it enables, most evidently of women, than Hulu's series, the adaptation of Margaret Atwood's *The Handmaid's Tale*. Living when our president unapologetically grabs "pussies," when Christian fundamentalism and biblical literalism remind us that God is watching the perverse, when there are daily diminishments to the checks and balances of a supposedly "democratic" governance, and when we know there are cameras everywhere, this show feels dead on, scarily so. Women's eyes are plucked out according to biblical injunction, while at the same time, every moment, every move may be witnessed, surveilled, by "the eyes." The show is so popular, I would venture, because it *feels* like it is the world, it manifests a world that is palpably true. Margaret Atwood's novel, published in 1985, the same year that Gary T. Marx invented the descriptor "surveillance society" (3), was dead center to Ronald Reagan's term as the US president. It is here adapted for Donald Trump's presidency. Both regimes were and are heinous threats to women. In *The Handmaid's Tale*, women who have somehow remained fertile in an ecologically poisoned world become reproduction machines, raped by one of the ruling patriarchs at the bottom edge of a bed while the handmaid's head is nestled into the crotch of the ruler's wife, between her spread legs, presumably providing the wife with some grotesque form of clitoral stimulation with each thrust while all three look dead, aghast, empty, hard. The only way that this subjection is possible is a totalized system of surveillance, which includes, like lynchings, bodies hung and left hanging, disobedient bodies given to be seen, even as the jutting white hoods of the handmaids restrict their peripheral vision, restrict their ability to look at all.

Leo Selvaggio's *URME Surveillance Identity Prosthetic*, 2014. Courtesy of the artist

Hulu's *The Handmaid's Tale*, 2017. Video Still: Courtesy of Hulu

While the handmaids in Atwood's novel are all white, the Hulu adaptation takes care to include black people. However, it appears to be working in a postrace (and post-class) mode. That is, there are no differentiations in the treatment of the women, or the assassinated men. Everyone is subject to surveillance equally, everyone equally at risk. In the series, the precataclysmic society we see in frequent flashbacks seems to be one of happy racial harmony. The central character Offred's best friend (Moira) is a black woman and Offred is married to a black man with whom she has a biracial child. In this pre- or verging on cataclysmic world there don't appear to be differentiations either. Bruce Miller, who adapted the novel and is the executive producer, says that the creative team decided to include "people of color" since, he says, in a world such as this, "fertility is the most precious resource, to be mined from whoever can provide it, regardless of race," and that "racism starts to fall" when people can't have kids and begin adopting from other countries. One could point out that the adoption of African and Asian babies can sometimes be exactly a differentiation based variously in race, racialized preferences, a white savior mentality, and calculations about the future success of those children. But nevertheless, in Miller's version of Atwood's surveillance society, racial differentiation doesn't exist. Race is simply no longer "visible." Instead, he says that in the "worldview" of the leaders of Gilead, "being a different color is not being a heretic. Believing something different is being a heretic."[3]

Throughout her carefully structured chapters, in which each study of an artist concludes with a detailed parsing of the way in which the artist may or may not have avoided reinscribing the effects or technologies of surveillance, Morrison is attentive to precisely that which Miller elides: the differentiations in surveillance and surveillance violence as it is applied to people of color, working-class or poor people, to gender and sexuality. She is to a certain extent consistently aware that, in effect, the eyes are white, that whiteness is the structural core of surveillance technology. But at the same time it is gender differentiation to which she wishes to pay special attention. She foregrounds the fact that her book is structured by a feminist frame and, in particular, second-wave feminism and materialist feminism. It is here that Morrison identifies her contribution to the field of surveillance studies. She writes that although scholars in the field have been identifying differential surveillance around race and class, the field is largely unattuned to the ways in which surveillance is gendered. She says that surveillance theorists, if anything, argue that men are now being surveilled just as much as women have always been. Although only one of her chapters, "Sex," concentrates almost exclusively on gender differentiations (and each of the chapters is titled with one word in an arresting counter to academia's long windedness: Stages, Streets, Screens, Sex, Skin, and Skies), Morrison returns repeatedly throughout the book to early feminist theory of the male gaze (which she notes is much complicated by "more interactive, agential social media")[4] and to foundational materialist feminist theater scholars such as Jill Dolan and Elin Diamond, as well as feminist theorists such as Hélène Cixous and Luce Iragaray.

For example, in "Screens," she discusses an online film called *I Love Alaska*. It was created via a "massive data leak in 2006" in which the Internet searches of 650,000 people could be accessed online by anyone. Identifiable as individuals by User Numbers, those people whose searches had been leaked could be and were traced and gathered into speculative histories and characteristics. The artists, Lernert Engelberts and Sander Plug, took up this opportunity and made a short film of thirteen episodes in which a voice-over lists various search queries originating from a single person. It is up to the "spectator" to sleuth through these queries to create plot and meaning. Morrison quotes Thomas Stubblefield: "The possibility of narrative coherence is contingent on the viewer's participation and mastery of relations of surveillance, his or her ability not only to successfully monitor and analyze an absent subject, but to mine this human-machine interaction for data."[5] Morrison's supplement to the commentary of others on this new form of dramaturgy and spectatorship is to say that they "risk overlooking a far more interesting dramaturgical structure within the film's material." She suggests that the film actually is structured around "the feminist self-representational strategy of [what Cixous called] *écriture feminine* rather than a traditional patriarchal cinematic narrative."[6] She suggests, fascinatingly, that User 711391 (who seemed ultimately to wish above all to go to Alaska) was not using her search engine solely as a middle-aged overweight somewhat desperate woman in lonely pursuit of information, as the filmmakers themselves framed it. Instead, she was writing onto or into the search engine in "a reflexive, circular mode of address that expresses not only alienation and loneliness but also resourcefulness, comfort and agency." She used Internet searches as "personal expressions of her desire and experience." This, Morrison says, is a version of Britta Sjogren's "voice-off" in which "the female voice can *speak for itself,* as it occupies an alternative space alongside . . . but elsewhere . . . [from] the image on the screen."[7] Morrison finds in this example a positive aspect of our participation in surveillance. She says, "we must remember that our individual screened lives are acts of creation and performance. And our usership, like time, like theater, is mutable, intersubjective, and full of loops and leaps."[8]

Morrison is concerned with redressing assumptions about gender neutrality in the surveilling eye, and discovering and critiquing surveillance-based art that reproduces, contests, and complicates it. Simone Brown, author of *Dark Matters: On the Surveillance of Blackness* (2015), offers a kind of parallel analysis. She is concerned that "within the field of surveillance studies race remains undertheorized" and stresses that "the historical formation of surveillance is not outside of the historical formation of slavery."[9] Morrison very specifically limits her study to surveillance art and performance from the twenty-first century; she wishes to convince her reader of the urgency of the production of this new genre. But Brown looks back, back to slavery as the originary site of technologies of surveillance, starting during the period that Nicholas Mirzoeff calls "The Plantation Complex," from 1660 to 1860. For Brown, blackness has always been surveilled, in technologies of what Mirzoeff calls "oversight,"[10] embodied in the overseer. In his book *The Right to Look: A Counterhistory of Visuality*, Mirzoeff provides a drawing from 1667 by Jean-Baptiste Du Tertre of an overseer in Jamaica, dressed in white, standing on a small elevated promontory "managing fourteen operations by visual surveillance alone."

If we follow Brown's look backward we can then imagine along with Foucault's prison an originary site of surveillance in slavery: in the overseer, the slave pen, the auction block, the Lantern Laws. We can allow this to resonate with Morrison's work. Mirzoeff even notes that it was during the same period, the mid-seventeenth century, that Foucault identified the emergence of the "order of things," and the Slave Code and the Code Noir were passed. These gave overseers the classifications by which to formalize surveillance. It might be possible to imagine this look backward from Morrison's contemporary performance site by thinking of it as not unlike the look backward from the small live-feed camera that the Iraqi artist Wafaa Bilal had implanted underneath the skin at the back of his skull for a year-long performance. The camera took a picture every minute and the images were sent to a website, available to the public, and to a gallery in Qatar. Morrison writes that, for Bilal, his body is "a stage" on which "to represent the brutal effects of . . . racial violence."[11] On one level Bilal meant the camera as a means by which to stress the level of surveillance by which we are surrounded. People walking behind him, for instance, would become aware of being watched from places that they do not expect and that are alarming. But on another level, the camera meant something else. Bilal writes that he "left many people and places behind," "places I was forced to leave behind and may never see again" and that *3rdi*, as the piece was

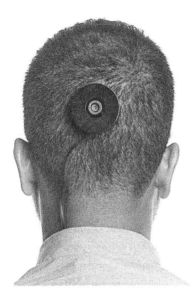

called, was a means by which to be able to "absorb" the "images" which, in the rush of his emergency leave-takings, "failed to fully register."[12] We could say, then, that to look back to the originary American site of surveillance is to be able to absorb fully the deep reality of racialized surveillance at the core and ongoing reality of this nation's experience, exactly that blind spot in Hulu's adaptation of *The Handmaid's Tale*. It could also, like Bilal's camera, register the succession of forced leave-takings that accompanied the black experience of movement under constant surveillance.

There is another moment of what I would call looking back in Morrison's book. It occurs early on in a section in which she describes the camera as the nineteenth-century technology that came to be depended on to provide evidence, the real, the truth, and is in that way the precursor of more contemporary forms of surveillance. Using Dion Boucicault's *The Octoroon*, she argues that Boucicault was "instruct[ing] his nineteenth-century audiences in the surveillant and evidentiary capabilities of photography."[13] She shows that especially the candid photograph, as opposed to the posed, came to be regarded as revealing the real. And then she uses Brandon Jenkins Jennings's adaptation of Boucicault's play to show that the evidentiary nature of the photograph can work as a counter gaze, a counter production of the truth, another form of looking back or, to use Mirzoeff's term, of "the right to look." She is talking here about the huge photograph of a lynching that drops suddenly into the scene at the height of the play's madcap melodrama and stops the show with its evidence of racial violence. This photograph is a real, historical image of a young black man's murder at the hands of white people. It supplements the theatricalized photograph accidentally taken in the play that proves the slave boy Paul's death at the hands not of Wah-no-tee (the "savage") but of M'Closky, the white villain.

Wafaa Bilal's *3rdi*, 2010–11. Courtesy of Wafaa Bilal and Mathaf, Arab Museum of Modern Art

Another example of looking back while being also in the present of the commodity form is Keith Obadike's "Black.net.art" called *Blackness for Sale*.[14] As Brown discusses it, Obadike was interested in the Internet trade in "Black Americana," including photographs of lynchings and instruments of slave torture sometimes described as family heirlooms. He decided to sell his blackness on eBay. The project was decidedly tongue-in-cheek. eBay pulled it after four days although Obadike intended it to go on for ten. He offered users the typical eBay site descriptions of the "product," albeit descriptions that were far from typical. He begins the description, for instance, by saying "This heirloom has been in the possession of the seller for twenty-eight years. Mr. Obadike's Blackness has been used primarily in the United States and its functionality outside of the US cannot be guaranteed. Buyer will receive a certificate of authenticity." This is followed by nine itemized suggestions for the use of his blackness including, for instance, "The seller does not recommend that this Blackness be used while voting in the United States of Florida."[15] Brown writes that Obadike saw the project as a "necessary counterframing to concurrent net.art in that it critiqued the commodification of blackness and the ways that colonial narratives are reproduced through Internet interfaces."[16]

Brown and Morrison explicitly converge in the coverage by each of biometrics. Brown, in the chapter "Branding Blackness," which also contains the example of Obadike, defines biometrics as "a technology of measuring the living body. The application of this technology is in the verification, identification, and automation practices that enable the body to function as evidence."[17] Morrison draws on Brown's use of the term "digital epidermalization."[18] Brown adds the "digital" to Franz Fanon's use of epidermalization, which she defines as "the imposition of race on the body."[19] She means by the addition to reference the ways that bodies are turned into digitalized code. In Morrison's work, biometrics is studied through the work of several artists who have created methods to block biometric recognition. These include Adam Harvey's *CV Dazzle*, Leonardo Selvaggid's URME mask series, and Manu Luksci's film *Faceless*. Morrison draws briefly on Brown's emphasis on the racializing effects of these technologies and stresses that biometrics is far from the neutrality it claims.

Not only in the section on biometrics, but throughout Morrison's book, there is a clear binary between technology and the human. Perhaps this is due to the way many surveillance artists are themselves framing it. In some ways, this "human" in opposition to technology assumes a white, privileged person with inalienable "rights" including the right to privacy. Looking back to the originary surveillance practice as technologies attenuated to slavery, including early forms of biometrics, helps us to complicate that binary. We have to consider that the object of the eye's gaze, the technological gaze, was not, exactly, the "human." Brown refers to Sylvia Wynter's concept of the "socio-genic principle," which "is understood as the organizational framework of our present human condition that names what is and what is not bounded within the category of the human, and that fixes and frames blackness as an object of surveillance."[20] That is, blackness stands outside the category of the human specifically as an object of surveillance. There is thus a stark difference between artists who perceive their work as an attempt at a recuperation of "humanity" and someone like Obadike, or Hank Willis Thomas. Thomas posted large photographs of a shaved black head branded with the Nike swoosh at bus stations and other public spots. He thus points to the ongoing commodification of blackness and black life in which blackness has always been a sur-veilled object circulating on the market. It is interesting that in *The Handmaid's Tale*, it is nonreproductive sexuality that is seized in the blind spot of the surveiller's gaze, when Offred makes love to a young man, one of the "eyes" in the house to which she is assigned. It is a kind of joy, or bliss, that is recuperated. Not individuality or privacy, not the "rights" of the human per se. Maybe it is not the human as a category that is the oppositional term to surveillance. Perhaps it never has been. Perhaps it is, as Morrison says, and I have quoted above, "acts of creation and performance . . . mutable, intersub-jective, and full of loops and leaps."

We live in and through highly differential, racialized and gendered technolo-gies, surveilled, and surveilling, that much is clear. In *The Handmaid's Tale*, there is no apparent technology. In fact, the rulers of this destroyed world believe in a return to older, simpler, nontechnological ways of doing things. The cook, for instance, has to make bread from scratch. Perhaps this is another reason the series feels so real, so recognizable, and as such is so popular. As Morrison says, surveillance works by pro-viding the signs and proofs of its watchfulness, but also through the unverifiability of its presence. There is a dis-ease that Offred seems to feel between watching the cook's bread making in the old-fashioned kitchen, motes of flour dust floating in the rays of sunlight slanting in through the old windows, in their old-fashioned fundamentalist clothing, (although organized by color in a kind of biometric organizing), and feeling/ knowing/but not seeing the presence of the eyes. In this dis-ease there is the damaging fundamentalism of "Americana," the pressure to live lives in the pretense of conven-tional markers of identity and to cooperate in surveillance while turning a blind eye to its presence, which we nevertheless know is there. Morrison, at the end of her book, encourages in the face of this dis-ease, the production of "small histories of surveil-lance." These she says will create "a constellation of alternative, humane, and intersub-jective pathways within surveillance society."[21] It is a useful starting point for describ-ing the impulses behind the work of the artists in Brown's and Morrison's books, and even in the postracial production that is Hulu's *The Handmaid's Tale*.

Notes

1. Elise Morrison, *Discipline and Desire: Surveillance Technologies in Performance* (Ann Arbor: University of Michigan Press, 2016), 268.

2. Ibid., 22.

3. Jessica Goldstein, "Hulu's 'The Handmaid's Tale' Shows How Diverse Casting Can Elevate a Classic," *ThinkProgress*, April 25, 2017, thinkprogress.org/making-dystopia-diverse-how-hulus-the-handmaid-s-tale-updates-the-classic-3e3f9f23401.

4. Morrison, *Discipline and Desire*, 181.

5. Ibid., 135, 137.

6. Ibid., 138.

7. Ibid., 139.

8. Ibid., 149.

9. Simone Brown, *Dark Matters: On the Surveillance of Blackness* (Durham, NC: Duke University Press, 2015), 8, 50.

10. Nicholas Mirzoeff, *The Right to Look: A Counterhistory of Visuality* (Durham, NC: Duke University Press, 2011), 10.

11. Morrison, *Discipline and Desire*, 222.

12. Ibid., 223.

13. Ibid., 94.

14. Ibid., 104.

15. Ibid., 107.

16. Ibid., 106.

17. Ibid., 109.

18. Morrison, *Discipline and Desire*, 192.

19. Brown, *Dark Matters*, 7.

20. Ibid.

21. Ibid., 275.

Printed and bound by CPI Group (UK) Ltd, Croydon, CR0 4YY